The Wheel Options Trading Strategy

A Proven Strategy For Creating Systematic, Repeatable, and Consistent Trading Profits

By Markus Heitkoetter

Table of Contents

IMPORTANT!

We had to print all illustrations in this book in black and white, otherwise the book would have cost us $40 to print

BUT...

... we have created a **Companion Guide** for you in which you can see all illustrations in color!

And the best: it's free!

Just go to WheelStrategyBook.com/bonus to download the companion guide for free.

And now, enjoy the book.

~Markus

Introduction

I love trading!

I've been doing it for basically half of my life at this point.

From what I've seen, traders aren't necessarily just one type of person. They come in all shapes, colors, and sizes. During my 20+ years following the markets, I don't think there's been any better time than now to be a trader.

I remember when I started trading, commissions were $40 per trade (!!!), and I had to pay $300 per month for real-time data.

Fast forward to today: Retail traders now have access to institutional-grade information and technology, making it easier and easier for just about anyone to start trading. And we now live in the age of "zero commissions", which makes it possible to take advantage of small moves in the markets without getting wiped out by commissions.

Over my career, I've traded just about everything you can. I've traded stocks, options, forex, and futures and as my life has changed, so has my trading style.

Now I'm 50 years old, and my priorities are much different than they were back in my early thirties. My kids are growing up and my time with them is really what's most important to me right now.

So I'm no longer trading strategies that require me to be in front of my computer for the majority of the day, and this is one of the many things I love about trading "The Wheel."

As you'll see, The Wheel is a great low management, high win rate strategy that will allow you to systematically, consistently, and repeatedly generate income while trading it.

So let's get rolling ;)

Chapter 1

3 Reasons Why You Must Start Trading TODAY

I'll be the first to admit it: trading can be a tough business. Trading may be one of the most difficult things you'll ever do. But just because something is difficult, doesn't mean it has to be complex.

I've worked with thousands of traders throughout my career, and the one thing it requires is discipline. The discipline to follow a plan, even when things get tough.

Because if you weren't aware of it, there are times when the market will (figuratively) kick your teeth in...and you need to be able to take it with a smile :)

Just like strikeouts are part of baseball, losses are part of trading. It's just that simple.

Trading has given me a life that some might think would never be possible for them, but I'm living proof that with determination, the right strategy, and mindset anyone can do this.

For me, there are three core reasons why you should trade and they're actually pretty simple:

Reason #1: You Can't Save Your Way To Financial Freedom

First, I hate to be the bearer of bad news, but you can't save your way to financial freedom!

There are people out there, financial experts even, who will make completely outlandish claims on how you can "save" your way to millionaire status.

One 'expert' in particular, Suze Orman, made such a claim in an article she wrote.

She said that you should simply stop buying coffee, and you can save your way to being a millionaire. Let's be honest, this is complete BS, and I will prove it to you:

Let's say you have $20,000 in your savings account and your goal is to save your way to $1,000,000 over the next 10 years.

Based on her advice, you'll need to stop drinking your daily latte to save that money.

But think about it: How much does a latte cost? Maybe $5?

So not spending $5 a day, over 30 days, would equal $150 a month in savings.

Let's assume you get an expected rate of return of 5% on your savings. And that is generous, because if you look at savings accounts or even CDs these days, you are lucky if you get 1%.

But let's assume that times will change and you get 5%.

At this rate of return it would take you 63 years and 5 months to save up to $1,000,000!

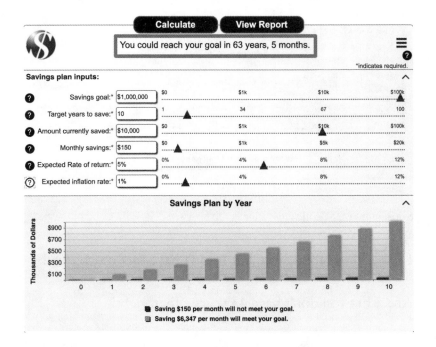

Source: https://dinkytown.net

So obviously, skipping the latte doesn't work.

Let's just say that in addition, you stop going out altogether and now you're saving a respectable $500 a month.

The good news, it would now "only" take you 43 years and 8 months to get to your goal of $1,000,000.

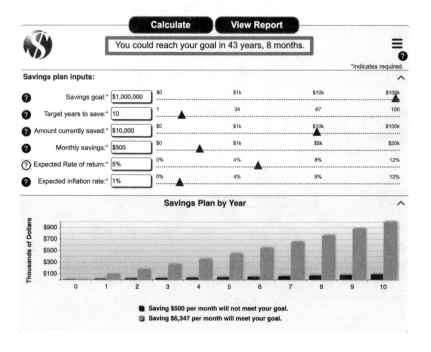

Source: https://dinkytown.net

I don't know about you, but I don't have that much time!

And I bet you don't have 43 years either, right?

So as you can see, you can't save your way to financial freedom.

You MUST find a way to make more money, and trading is a perfect way to do this.

"If you don't find a way to make money while you sleep, you will work until you die. - Warren Buffett"

Reason #2: Trading is The Ultimate Equal Opportunity Playing Field

Trading is the ultimate equal opportunity playing field.

When you're trading, it doesn't matter who you are.

It doesn't matter whether you are young or old. It doesn't matter whether you are a man or a woman. It doesn't matter if you are white, black, brown, green, or pink. It doesn't matter if you are a math genius, or you need a calculator to add two numbers together, as I do. As you know, if you watch my videos on YouTube, then you know that I use a calculator for everything! It certainly doesn't matter if you are a Ph.D., or whether or not you dropped out of high school.

You see, trading is the ultimate equal opportunity 'employer'. With trading, there is no discrimination. In all areas of life, there IS discrimination, whether we like it or not, but NOT in trading.

With trading, it's not men vs. women, or young vs. old.

There is only the educated vs. the uneducated.

The ones that win are the ones that have the right system, the ones that have the right mindset, and the right tools. They are the ones who are trading against the gamblers, and I think we know which group usually wins, right?

As you can see, trading is the ultimate playing field, and this is one of the many reasons why I love it!

Reason #3: Money Can't Buy Happiness? - WRONG!

When trading, you can make money… and money CAN buy happiness!

I know, I know: This is a controversial statement, because a lot of people say - and unfortunately, believe - that "money can't buy you happiness."

Well… based on my experience, they are dead WRONG, and as always, I will prove it to you!

Recently, I set up a smaller account of $50,000 to prove how profitable "The Wheel Strategy" can be. After a month of trading "The Wheel", the realized profit in this account was $3,204.

And I chose to use these profits to prove how money can buy happiness.

Let me ask you: do you know someone who is in a tough spot right now?

Maybe you know someone who has been laid off, and can't pay their rent anymore, or maybe somebody who has gotten sick, and can't pay for the medication?

If you answered "yes" to any of these questions, then let me ask you this:

What if you could give them the $3,204 I mentioned? Do you think this could change the life of someone who is in a tight spot?

Well, very recently, I decided to give away that month's worth of profits to a few people in need.

I had our members and viewers nominate someone they knew, who was currently having a tough time. I reviewed the (heart-wrenching) submissions, picked the two candidates who I felt could use it the most, and I split the profits from this trading account and sent them a check.

It helped them out a great deal, and it meant the world to them.

So for me, this was pretty simple proof that money CAN buy happiness, and can change your - and other's - life for the better.

Take a look at these smiles:

In my personal experience, trading is the best way to make more money.

Money can change your life for the better and also the lives of those around you, and I'll show you how to do it with The Wheel Strategy.

I will show you the tools that you need, and I'll give you the strategy that I personally use, and we'll also talk about the right mindset of a trader.

There will be no hype in this book, just the facts.

Because I want you to succeed.

Chapter **2**

Why "The Wheel" Is The Perfect Trading Strategy

I want to give you a super quick summary of what inspired me to write this book.

I see it all the time: People who start trading expect their accounts to explode.

After all, that's what all these ads and emails promise:

Insane returns in just a few days!

"Make 1,062% with this stock."

"Turn $500 into $2,000,000 in 2 years!"

… or something crazy like that.

And then they start trading, and they quickly realize: it doesn't work this way.

If you are sick of all this hype and empty promises, then THIS strategy and book are for you.

My goal is to give you a strategy, and the tools that you will need to grow your account systematically - because that is the key.

You see, everybody can get lucky now and then and have a winning trade that makes a lot of money. But being able to grow your account in a systematic, and repeatable way...that is the key to long-term success in the markets.

When people first start trading The Wheel and it really 'clicks', they are pleasantly surprised by the high win rate and how easy it is to manage a trade.

It simply comes down to following the simple rules I'll lay out in this book, along with choosing good stocks that you don't mind owning.

For me, a trading strategy must be **systematic, consistent, and repeatable**, and "The Wheel Strategy" checks all of these boxes.

Who Should Trade This Strategy?

This strategy is perfect for beginners.

It's also a fantastic strategy if you have a portfolio or a retirement account that isn't growing at least 30% per year (like many IRA and 401k accounts).

"The Wheel Strategy" is also perfect as an add-on strategy for those who already have a "bread and butter" strategy, like my core growth strategy, **The PowerX Strategy.**

The Wheel is used by both retail and institutional traders.

In fact, one of the most well-known investors of all time, Warren Buffett, deploys this strategy as a way to generate income while he's waiting to buy stocks at the prices he wants.

And you can also use this strategy to generate weekly and monthly income.

In short, if you have some money and are looking for a consistent way to grow your account, then THIS strategy is for you.

What Are The Pros Of Using This Strategy?

First and foremost, this strategy has a very high winning percentage.

The Wheel Strategy is a high probability strategy with around a 90-95% win rate, making it tough to lose when implemented properly.

In fact, over the summer and fall of 2020, I went on one of my longest, if not the longest, winning streaks ever.

Over roughly a 5-month period and 70+ trades, I didn't have a single losing trade with The Wheel.

Does this mean you shouldn't expect losses? NO!

There will be losses, but The Wheel is a strategy with such a high win rate that it's common to see long-standing win streaks without any losses.

Another advantage of this strategy is the extremely low time requirement:

It doesn't require hours upon hours of analysis, so you don't have to sit in front of your computer all day.

All you need is about 15 minutes or less a few times a week.

Let me prove it to you:

During the Summer of 2020, I took a trip to Germany with my two kids to visit my family.

No matter if it was on a plane, train, or Uber, I was still able to implement this strategy while on the go.

In fact, I was able to close out a few trades while on the plane, at around 36,000 ft. up in the sky, using the crappy WiFi that you typically experience on planes.

Check it out:

Here's another advantage:

When implemented correctly, it is a rather 'safe' trading strategy.

The goal of The Wheel Strategy is to produce at least an annual return on your capital of 30% (or 60% with a margin account).

When trading, losses are a part of this business, but this strategy is designed to minimize these losses by doing our due diligence when choosing stocks to trade, making it a relatively safe strategy to use.

No matter what strategy you decide to trade, you must fully grasp and realize that there is no 'reset' button in trading.

So before you ever place a trade, you should fully understand the risks of the strategy you're trading.

You should never - and I mean NEVER - trade with money you can't afford to lose.

The Basic Idea Of The Wheel Strategy

Over the next few chapters, you will learn all the details about this strategy. But let me give you the 30,000-ft overview right now.

The basic idea is to get **paid while you wait** to buy stocks at a price you're willing to own them at.

Here's how:

1. You sell Put Options and **collect premiums**. This premium gets deposited in your account, and this results in weekly or monthly 'paychecks'.

2. When a stock price closes below the Put Option strike price at expiration, you will be assigned 100 shares of stock per option that you sold. You will still keep the premium you received as the option writer.

3. Once you own shares, "The Wheel" gets its momentum: You begin to sell 1 Call Option for every

100 shares that you own and **get more premium,** resulting in more weekly or monthly income.

4. If the stock price closes below the Call Option strike price at expiration, then you simply keep the premium for the Calls sold against your shares and **repeat this process.**

5. If the stock price closes above the Call Option strike price at expiration, you sell your shares at the strike price and **make money on the shares**. Now you don't own any more shares, and you start this process again.

This strategy is reliable, time tested, and very low maintenance.

As you can see, you can <u>systematically</u> earn money trading The Wheel without spending hours and hours a day in front of your computer stressing over what you should trade.

Chapter 3

Trading For A Living

There are two levels in trading:

1. **Trading For Growth**
   Most traders start here. In this phase, your goal is to grow a small account into a bigger one so that you can move to the next level.

2. **Trading For Income**
   When you are trading for income, your account is large enough so that you no longer have to grow it. In this phase, you would regularly wire your trading profits into your checking account to cover your living expenses.

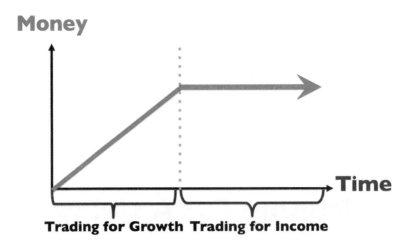

Trading for Growth Trading for Income

In this chapter, I will explain these levels in more detail so you know which stage you are currently at, and how to use The Wheel Strategy correctly.

So first, we'll start with trading for growth as most people start with a smaller account, e.g. less than $200,000.

Trading For Growth

Most traders start with a trading account smaller than $200,000, and that's ok!

If this is true for you, then you're "trading for growth".

At this level, the idea is simple: Keep growing your account until you are at a level where you can comfortably trade for income without breaking the rules of your trading strategy.

I typically recommended starting with no less than $5,000, but ideally you're able to start with at least $10,000.

When trading for growth, the strategy that you use should have at least a 50% ROI per year.

The focus of this book is to teach you The Wheel Strategy which requires an account size of at least $20,000.

If your account is currently less than $20,000, I recommend trading "The PowerX Strategy" instead of The Wheel.

The PowerX Strategy allows you to grow a small account into a larger one using Money Management.

I have written a book on this strategy that can be found on Amazon, or you can pick it up on our website for FREE, all you need to do is pay for shipping and handling.

So if you've just read this section and you're realizing that The Wheel might not be the right strategy for you just yet... don't be discouraged. Keep reading! Because The Wheel Strategy is basically three strategies in one, and you will learn a lot of key fundamentals that you can utilize while still at the growth trading level.

Trading For Income

So what is the difference between "trading for growth" vs. "trading for income"?

"Trading for income" means that your trading account is large enough to trade and wire profits that will supplement or replace your income. But "large enough" will depend on your goals and the ROI expectations of the strategy that you are trading.

Let me give you an example:

Let's say that you have $500,000 worth of buying power in your trading account, and you are using The Wheel Strategy.

The goal of The Wheel Strategy is to generate an ROI of 30%, so this would be $150,000 per year in profits.

That's $12,500 a month.

So when you are trading for income, after a set amount of time, whether it's once a month or once a quarter, you will transfer any amount greater than $500,000 out of your trading account into your checking account.

It's important to understand that your account size is probably the biggest factor when determining if you're ready to start trading for income.

As shown in my example above, it really comes down to a simple formula:

The more buying power you have in your account, the greater your earning potential.

How Much Money Do You Need To Trade For A Living?

So how do you know if your trading account is big enough to begin trading for income?

Well, this number will vary widely from person to person.

Determining what your income goal should be really depends on a few different factors:

- What are your monthly living expenses?

- How many dependents rely on your income?

- What additional income do you need, e.g. to buy cool stuff like cars and boats?

These are just a few examples of what should be taken into account when figuring out how much income you need to generate every month.

And as boring as this sounds, it helps to make a budget. You don't have to account for everything, but you should list your major expenses, e.g:

- Housing (25-35%): mortgage, insurance, taxes, maintenance

- Transportation (10-15%): payments or lease, insurance, gas, repairs

- Food (10-15%): groceries, restaurants

- Utilities (5-10%): gas, water, power, internet, TV, phone

- Insurances & healthcare (10-15%): health insurance, life insurance, co-pays

- Travel and Entertainment (10-20%)

Once you arrive at a number and know exactly how much income you must make every month, there's a simple formula that you can use to calculate how much you should have in your trading account so that you can generate this amount of money every month.

The formula is:

Buying Power In Your Trading Account = Desired Annual Income / Expected ROI

Here are some examples:

Let's say you want to make $10,000 per month, i.e. $120,000 per year, and you are using a strategy with an ROI of 60% (such as the PowerX Strategy).

Here is how you would figure out how much buying power you need in your trading account:

$120,000 Desired Annual Income / 0.6 Expected ROI = $200,000

So you would need $200,000 in buying power in your trading account.

And if this account were a margin account, you would only need $100,000 in cash, since a margin account doubles your buying power.

Let's look at another example:

Let's say you want to earn $6,000 per month = $72,000 per year.

And let's assume you are using a strategy with an ROI of 30% (such as The Wheel Strategy).

Here's the formula:

$72,000 Desired Annual Income / 0.3 Expected ROI = $240,000

So you need $240,000 in buying power in your account, and if you are trading a margin account, you would need $120,000 in cash to make $6,000 per month.

As you can see, it's quite easy to calculate the money you need in your trading account to trade for a living. What's YOUR number?

The Most Important Key Metric For Income Traders

When trading for income, you need to treat it like you would any business. And with any successful business, you need to keep an eye on key metrics that reflect the overall health of their business.

For an income trader, there is ONE key metric you must always be aware of.

Can you guess what it is?

Believe it or not, it's NOT the winning percentage. It is not the profit factor.

And it's also not the average profit per trade.

The most important metric is a number that you might have never even heard about before because not many traders talk about it.

The most important metric when trading for income is the **Profit Per Day (PPD).**

When trading for income, you need to be able to forecast at what pace you are making money.

Yes, of course, it is important how much money you make.

But there's a huge difference if you make $1,000 in a day or in a month!

Because when trading for income, you need consistency. You need to be able to reasonably predict how much money you will make over a month or quarter.

And that's why PPD is the most important metric when trading for income using The Wheel Strategy. Knowing your PPD gives you the ability to quickly know if the trades you have in your account are keeping you on track to hitting your income goals.

Generating SRC Profits

No matter if you're trading for income or for growth, you must find a way to generate what I call **"SRC Profits"**.

SRC Profits are trading profits that are generated in a Systematic, Repeatable, and Consistent way (SRC).

And here's why SRC profits are so important:

Everybody can get lucky every now and then. If you are trading long enough, you will get a "lucky trade".

Take the AAPL stock split in August 2020 as an example:

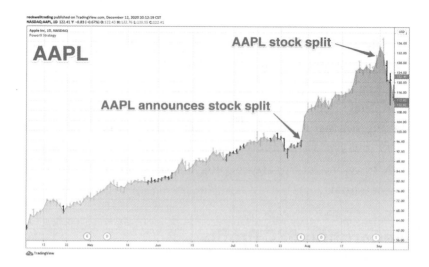

During its Earnings Call on July 30, 2020, Apple announced a 4:1 stock split for August 31, 2020.

And after the announcement, **Apple rallied 30% in 4 weeks!**

If you caught this move, good for you!

However, these are <u>not</u> SRC Profits, and here's why:

This wasn't systematic, because there was no plan, no strategy, nothing that went through any sort of testing that deemed it an effective method for making money in the markets.

It was simply a 'roll of the dice'.

This was also not repeatable.

You don't know when the next AAPL split is going to happen.

And we have no way to accurately predict the direction the stock will head right before or after the split takes place.

In fact, as you can see from the chart below, over the next 3 months the AAPL stock didn't go anywhere and was just trading sideways:

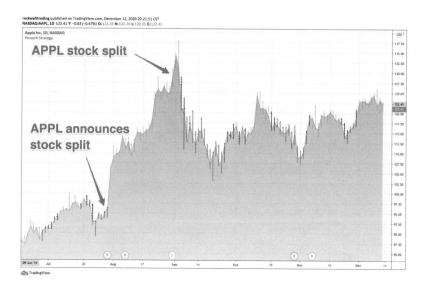

Let me give you another example:

Some people got lucky when they bought ZOOM (ZM) during the Coronavirus pandemic.

Between February and October 2020, ZM shot up 564%!

And again: if you caught this move, or even just part of the move: good for you!

But this is another great example of a "lucky trade".

Because you won't be able to repeat this trade next month… or next year.

If you caught it, it was probably the trade of the century, and you won't be able to do it again.

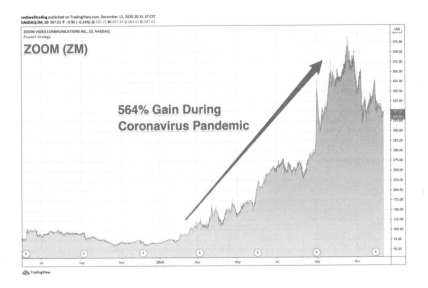

As a professional trader, you don't want to rely on "lucky trades".

If they happen, they are the "cherry on top". These are the trades that allow you to buy a new car - or helicopter.

But for your income trading, you need SRC Profits.

All of my trading strategies are systematic, repeatable, and consistent. SRC Profits are absolutely crucial when trading for a living.

And that is why I only use strategies like "The Wheel" that can produce SRC Profits, week in and week out.

Chapter 4

Options 101 - Here's What You Need To Know

*"Get the fundamentals down and the level
of everything you do will rise."*

~ Michael Jordan

The Wheel is an options trading strategy.

So before you can start trading The Wheel, you first need to understand the basics of options.

This chapter is perfect for you if you are new to options because I promise that I will make it easy to understand options without filling you full of useless jargon.

This chapter is also great if you have some experience with options, but maybe find them a bit confusing, and aren't sure how all this works.

Most people who try to teach someone about options like to overcomplicate it.

They talk about things like The Black Scholes Model or The Binomial Model, "The Greeks" like Delta, Theta, Rho, implied volatility, etc.

And they like to throw out fancy terms to make options trading sound VERY complicated - and to sell you their courses.

But that's not me. That has never been my style.

I like to keep things as simple as possible.

There's a quote by Einstein that encapsulates this perfectly:

"Everything Should Be Made as Simple as Possible, But Not Simpler."

If you are brand new to options trading, there are a lot of rabbit holes you can go down.

The good news: To trade The Wheel you just need to understand a few of the basics, and then you'll have all the knowledge and confidence you need to start trading it.

So in this chapter, we are going to discuss the basics and focus on just what you need for a rock-solid options foundation.

What Is An Option?

An option is a contract that gives you the right, but not the obligation, to buy or sell 100 shares of a stock or ETF, at a specific price, by a certain date.

The difference between stocks and options: A stock represents ownership of a company. And an option is just a contract that you can use to buy or sell those shares.

There are advantages to buying options, instead of just buying the actual shares of the stock outright.

Keep in mind that ONE options contract represents the right to buy 100 shares.

If you were to buy 100 shares of AAPL, you have to pay the actual share price of the stock multiplied by 100. So if AAPL's stock is trading for $126/share, then 100 shares would cost $12,600.

However, if you buy 1 option contract, you are paying a fraction of that price to control the same amount of shares.

AAPL	IV Rank 24.9	Last X Size 126.66 Q 67.4M	Chg -2.04	Bid X 127.29 P	Ask X 127.32 Q

| TRADE MODE | | | | | STRATEGY |
| TABLE | CURVE | ACTIVE | GRID | PAIRS | ANALYSIS | LONG |

	▫ Theo	▫ Last	Bid	Ask	Strike
▲ Jan 8, 2021 W				Calls	19d
	5.41	5.10	5.00	5.20	125
	4.83	4.65	4.45	4.65	126
	4.30	4.05	3.95	4.10	127
	3.81	3.65	3.40	3.65	128
	3.34	3.15	3.05	3.20	129
	2.92	2.79	2.60	2.79	130

Here's an example:

As you can see in the image above, the option to buy AAPL at $126 costs $4.65.

Since options trades in "100 packs", you would pay $465 for the right to buy AAPL for $126 on or before January 8th, 2021, which is 19 days from now.

Would you rather pay $12,600 to own 100 shares of AAPL at $126, or $465 for the right to buy AAPL at $126?

Obviously, it's cheaper to buy the RIGHT to own AAPL for $465 than buying 100 shares of AAPL outright.

Another advantage:

When buying options, there is limited downside risk. If you buy shares of a company outright, and the price plummets, you can lose as much as 100% of the investment if the price drops to $0.

Now that is an unlikely scenario, but it's still a possibility. Does anyone remember Enron or Worldcom?

When buying options, you don't have the *obligation* but rather the *right* to follow through on the trade, and if you don't, you've only lost out on the amount you paid for the contract.

Using the example above, you can never lose more than $465, even if AAPL shares would plummet to $76.

If you traded 100 shares, you would lose $126 - $76 = $50 * 100 shares = $5,000.

But if you traded the option, you would only lose $465.

When selling options, there's a bit more risk involved, and we will cover this in a moment.

4 Things You Need To Know About Options

Now that you have a basic idea of what an option is, there are 4 things you need to know about them, and these are universal:

1. Options have a Strike Price.

2. Options have an Expiration Date.

3. There are Call Options, and there are Put Options.

4. You can buy options, or you can sell options.

So let's take a look at these 4 things in more detail.

#1 - Strike Prices

The strike price is the price that the underlying asset (in this example stock) can be purchased at if the option contract is exercised. You'll choose the strike price at the time of purchase or when the option contract is written.

Which strike you choose and the price of the stock at the time of purchase will determine if your strike is considered In-The-Money (ITM), At-The-Money (ATM), or Out-Of-The-Money (OTM).

In-The-Money Options Strike Prices (ITM)

ITM Call Options will have strike prices below the current stock price. And ITM Put Options, will have strike prices above the current stock price.

For our AAPL example (Current price $126.66), the strike prices of 125 and below are considered ITM for Call options. And the strike prices of 128 and above are considered ITM for Put options.

At-The-Money Options Strike Price (ATM)

An ATM option would be the closest strike price to the current market price of the stock.

For our AAPL example (Current price $126.66), the strike prices of 126 and 127 are the closest strikes to the market. So these strikes are considered ATM for both Call and Put options.

Out-Of-The-Money Options Strike Prices (OTM)

An OTM Call Option's strike price would be above the current market price of the stock. With an OTM Put Option, the strike price would be below the current market price of the stock.

For our AAPL example (Current price $126.66), the strike prices of 128 and above are considered OTM for Call options.

And the strike prices of 125 and below are considered OTM for Put options.

#2 - Expiration Dates

Options are contracts that will always have an expiration date.

All options have <u>monthly expiration dates</u>, and some options also have <u>weekly expiration dates</u>.

The weekly expiration dates are often marked with a "w":

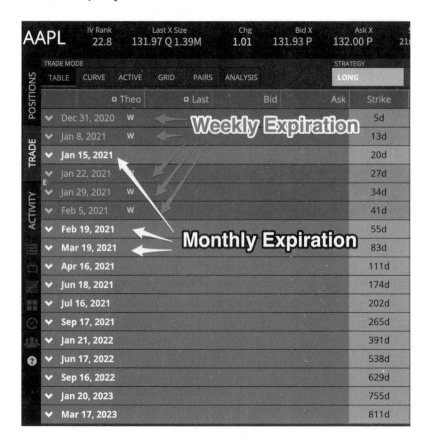

The expiration date is always specified as a Friday, unless it's a major holiday like Christmas 2020, which fell on Friday, December 25th. In this case, the expiration is the day before the holiday.

Once an option expires, you no longer have the right to buy or sell the underlying stock at the specified strike price.

Therefore, it is very important that you choose the right expiration date.

As an option BUYER, you want a longer expiration date, usually 30 days or more.

As an option SELLER, you want a shorter expiration date, usually 14 days or less.

We will talk more about that in the next chapter.

#3 - Call Options vs. Put Options

There are call options and there are put options.

Let's take a look at both options in more detail:

<u>Call Options</u>

In the previous chapters, we talked mainly about Call Options.

As a reminder: When you own a call option, you have the right to buy a stock at the Strike Price before the expiration. So if the option has a Strike Price of $100, and the actual price of the stock goes up to $110, you get to buy the stock at $100 a share instead of $110 a share.

Often, you will see a Call notated like this: "AAPL Call 280 April 17".

This means that you can buy AAPL for $280 (Strike Price) on or before April 17th (expiration). Remember, you have the right to do this, but not the obligation. Let's take a look at a chart and see if this makes sense.

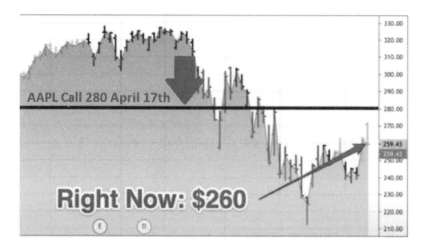

For this example, let's assume AAPL is trading at $260.

If you own the AAPL Call 280 April 17, it means we have the right to buy AAPL for $280 before April 17th.

Quiz: How much is the option worth if AAPL is trading at $260, and you have the right to buy AAPL at $280?

The answer is "nothing"!

This Call Option is "out of the money."

It wouldn't make sense to exercise this Call Option and buy the shares for $280 when it is cheaper to just buy the stock outright at $260.

This Call Option would only be worth something if the stock moved above $280. But as long as the price of the stock remains below $280, the Call Option is worth nothing.

Let's take a look at another example with a different strike price:

Here is a different Strike Price.

This is the AAPL Call 240 April 17. In this example, you have the right, but not the obligation, to buy AAPL at the Strike Price of $240 on or before the expiration of April 17th.

In the chart above, AAPL is currently trading at $260.

Same question here: How much is the Call Option worth?

Well, if you are allowed to buy the stock at $240, and it is currently trading at $260, that means the Call Option is worth $20 - and it's "in the money."

It really is that simple. The Strike Price vs. the current price the stock is trading at determines the value of the Call Option.

If the Strike Price is lower than the current price the stock is trading at, then it is "in the money."

On the other hand, if the Strike Price is higher than the current price the stock is trading at, then it is "out of the money."

But there's a kicker:

There is also something else to consider, and that's what's known as **Time Value**.

We will go over Time Value in more detail in the next chapter, but I want to briefly cover it here first, as it is a basic principle of options trading.

Right now, this option is trading at $22.30.

But wait…. If this Call Option is worth $20, as we've just established, why is it trading for more than $20? Why is there a so-called "Premium" there?

This Premium is also commonly referred to by traders as "Time Value." In this case, it could be because the price of AAPL is moving even higher, and this is what traders are anticipating because there is a certain amount of days left where we are allowed to buy this stock for $240. As the price of AAPL moves higher, it will be worth more.

The Premium you see is only the Premium for one share, and since each contract represents 100 shares, this number multiplied by 100 is the amount in the Premium you will pay.

As long as there's still time left before expiration, options always have some Time Value, in addition to the real value. More about that in the next chapter.

Put Options

At this point, you should have a good grasp of what Call Options are.

But we've only briefly discussed what a Put Option is, so let's talk about this in more detail now.

A Call Option gives you the right to **buy** a stock at a certain price before the expiration date. And a Put Option gives you the right to **sell** a stock at a certain price (Strike Price) before the expiration.

Here's an example: AAPL Put 280 April 17.

This Put Option allows you to sell AAPL for $280 (Strike Price), before April 17th (expiration). Remember, you have the right to do this, but not the obligation, just like with Call Options.

With AAPL trading at $260, you have the right to sell the stock at the much higher price of $280 (when you sell stock you profit from a falling market). This means that the Put Option is worth $20 - and it is "in the money."

#4 - Buying Options vs Selling Options

When buying options, you either have the right to buy or sell the underlying security at a specified price (the strike price), depending on whether Calls or Puts were purchased.

Buying options is considered a 'debit' since you're paying upfront for the contract.

When selling options, you are taking the other side:

You have either the obligation to buy or sell the underlying security at a specified price (the strike price), once again dependent on if Calls or Puts were sold.

When selling options, you're receiving a 'credit' in the form of the premium for the contract you sold.

There are two key concepts to take away when buying options or selling options.

First, when buying options you have the **right** to buy or sell the shares of the underlying security. Also, when buying options you're paying upfront which is considered a **debit**.

When selling options, you have the **obligation** to buy or sell shares of the underlying security. When you're the option writer (selling options) you're collecting a fee for selling that contract, referred to as a **'credit'**.

Let's take a look at this in more detail:

Buying Options

➡Rockwell TRADING	Calls	Puts
Buying	When Buying Calls You Have The RIGHT To BUY A Security At A Specified Price	When Buying Puts You Have The RIGHT To SELL A Security At A Specified Price

When you buy a Call Option, you make money when the stock goes up.

Example: If the option has a Strike Price of 100, and the price of the stock rises to $110, you can buy stock priced at $110 a share, for only $100 a share.

However, if the price drops below the Strike Price, you don't have the obligation to follow through on the trade. So your maximum loss is the premium you paid for the options contract.

Remember, when buying options you have the RIGHT, not the OBLIGATION to exercise a contract, so you don't have to buy the shares.

When you buy a Put Option, you make money when the stock goes down.

Example: If the option has a Strike Price of 110, and the price of the stock drops to $100, this means you can sell shares that only cost you $100 a share, for the higher price of $110 a share.

However, if the price rises above the Strike Price, you don't have the obligation to follow through on the trade, and again, you will only be down the price of the premium you paid.

Remember, with buying options, you only have the right, not the obligation to exercise the contract.

Selling Options

≫Rockwell TRADING	Calls	Puts
Selling	When Selling Calls You Have The OBLIGATION To SELL A Security At A Specified Price	When Selling Puts You Have The OBLIGATION To BUY A Security At A Specified Price

There are always two sides to every trade: Whenever a trader buys a Call, or a Put, there is someone on the other end selling that Call, or Put to them.

So when the buyer pays a premium for an option, the seller of that contract collects that premium.

And that's exactly what we will do with "The Wheel Strategy".

Just think about it as "doing the opposite":

When you **sell a Call Option**, you make money when the price goes **down**.

When you sell a Call Option, you receive a premium. And if you sold a Call Option with a Strike Price of 260, and the price of the stock closed <u>below</u> $260 at expiration, this option would expire worthless and you would keep the premium.

However, if the price rises above $260, let's say $280, you still collect the Premium, but you now have the obligation to sell the shares at the Strike Price - IF the buyer exercises their right to buy the shares at the Strike Price.

This is called "assignment," or "getting assigned," and is a big part of The Wheel Strategy. We will cover this in more detail in Chapter 8.

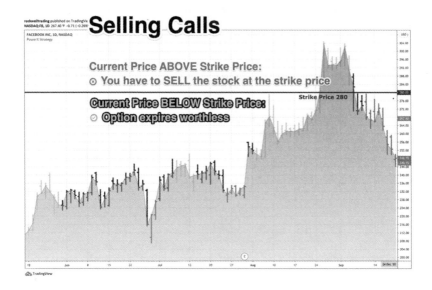

In this example, you would lose $20 per option: You have to sell the shares at the strike price of 260, but since you don't have the shares, you need to buy them at the higher price of 280 for a loss of $20.

When you **sell a Put Option**, you make money when the price goes up - or as long as the stock price stays above the strike that you sold.

If you sold a put option that has a Strike Price of $280, and the price of the stock closes above $280 at expiration, the option expires worthless and you keep the entire Premium the buyer paid.

However, if the price drops below $280, let's say to $250, you still collect the Premium, but you now have the

OBLIGATION to buy shares at the Strike Price (the process is known as assignment).

So you would lose $30 per share if you had the obligation to buy shares at $280 and immediately sold them at $250 (current market price) to close the trade. And since options come in "100-packs", you would lose 100 * $30 = $3,000.

Four (4) Options Strategies - Your Building Blocks

Now that you have a solid foundation in options trading, I want to show you 4 basic options strategies. These 4 strategies are the "building blocks" of options trading.

Once you understand these 4 foundational strategies, you will then be able to build more advanced and complex trading strategies.

We will use 2 out of these 4 strategies when trading "The Wheel."

So here are the 4 basic strategies for trading options:

1. Buy Calls - When you expect the stock to go up (Bullish).

2. Sell Calls - When you expect the stock to go sideways or drop (Bearish).

3. Buy Puts - When you expect the stock to drop (Bearish).

4. Sell Puts - When you expect the stock to go sideways or go up (Bullish).

As you can see, there's more than one way you can take advantage of moves higher and lower in the market.

So the question then becomes:

When would you use one of these strategies over another?

If you are bullish and expect the price of the stock to go up, you would either **buy Calls** or **sell Puts**.

If, on the other hand, you are bearish and expect the price of the stock to drop down, you would either **sell Calls** or **buy Puts**.

A good way for you to determine whether to buy or sell options is to refer to the CBOE Volatility Index (VIX) - also known as "The Fear Index."

The VIX was created by the Chicago Board Options Exchange (CBOE) and is a real-time market index that represents the market's expectation of 30-day forward-looking volatility.

In a nutshell, when the VIX is high, it's typically better to SELL options. When the VIX is high, option premiums are also going to be higher. And when option premiums are high, you collect more premium as a seller.

And when the VIX is low, it's better to BUY options since the premiums will be lower.

As a basic rule of thumb, when the VIX is above 30, you SELL options. And when it is below 30, you want to BUY options.

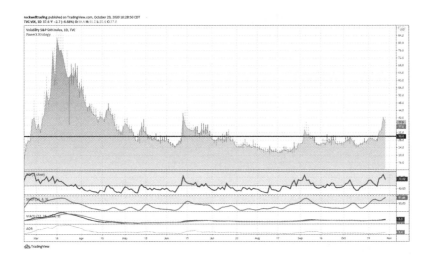

As you can see, trading options doesn't have to be overly complicated.

You just need the basics that we discussed in this chapter to start trading options. What you have learned thus far is all you need for The Wheel.

But...and yes, there is a big BUT coming... Trading options can be dangerous if you don't know what you're doing!

This is why I included this chapter that focused just on the fundamentals of trading options.

A lot of people lose their hard-earned money trading options because they don't understand these basics.

And even if you are still a little bit confused, that's okay.

Keep reading, and if you get stuck later on, then you may want to reread this chapter a couple of times.

And that's OK because once you do get it, you've got it!

Chapter 5

Understanding Premium & Theta Decay

In this chapter, we're going to cover Premium and Theta Decay in more detail.

We'll go through specific examples of how they work and as you'll see, Theta Decay and the collection of Premium are key parts of The Wheel strategy.

Premium With Call Options

Here's an example:

Let's say a stock is currently trading at $132.

And let's say we are looking at a Call Option with a Strike Price of 125 and another Call Option with a Strike Price of 135.

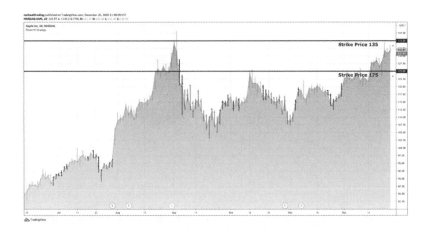

When we buy a Call Option with a Strike Price of 135, we have the right to buy the stock for $135.

Of course, we wouldn't exercise this right. Because it doesn't make sense to buy the stock at 135 (the strike price), when the current price is $132.

And that's why the REAL VALUE, or intrinsic value, of this option is $0. That's very typical for an "out of the money" option.

On the other hand, the Call Option with a Strike Price of 125 is a different story.

A Strike Price of 125 means we can buy the stock for $125. So we could "exercise the option", own the stock for $125 and sell it right away at the current price of $132.

This means that the real value of this call is $132 - $125 = $7. And this option is referred to as "in the money."

But if we look at the options chain, we see that this option with 20 days to expiration (DTE) is currently trading at $8.75!

AAPL	IV Rank 22.8	Last X Size 131.97 Q 1.39M	Chg 1.01	Bid X 131.93 P	Ask X 132.00 P	21

	TRADE MODE					STRATEGY		
	TABLE	CURVE	ACTIVE	GRID	PAIRS	ANALYSIS	**LONG**	

	▫ Theo	▫ Last	Bid	Ask	Strike
▲ **Jan 15, 2021**				Calls	20d
	8.76	8.75	8.70	8.80	125
	8.05	8.00	8.00	8.10	126
	7.36	7.25	7.30	7.40	127
	6.70	6.69	6.65	6.75	128
	6.06	6.07	6.05	6.15	129

We already established the real (or intrinsic) value of this option:

The Stock Price: $132 - The Strike Price: $125 = $7

The difference between the current market price and the real value is what's known as the Time Value. So the Time Value of this Call Option is:

Market Price $8.75 - Real Value $7 = Time Value $1.75

So what exactly is "Time Value"?

Traders are expecting the price of the stock to move higher between now and expiration, and that's why they are willing to pay a premium for the option. The Time Value (also known as Premium) that traders are willing to pay for an option will get smaller every day.

On the day of expiration, the time value of $1.75 will have decreased to only a few cents.

Premium With Put Options

Let's use the same example with Put Options.

The stock is trading at $132.

And we are considering Put Options with a strike price of $135 and $125:

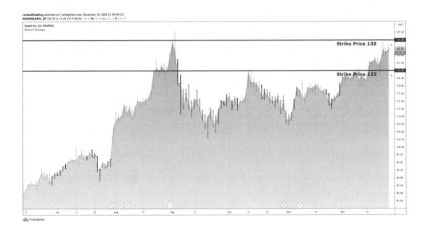

When buying **Call Options**, we can **buy** the stock at the Strike Price.

But when buying **Put Options**, we can **sell** a stock at the Strike Price.

In this case, the strike price of 125 is "out of the money" and has no real value.

Here's why: The Put Option with a strike price of 125 gives us the right to **sell** the stock at $125. But if we sold the stock outright, without using an option, we could sell it for $132 right now!

Just to clarify: when buying, we will profit when we can buy at a lower price and sell higher. When selling, we will profit when we can sell at a higher price and buy lower.

On the other hand, the strike price of $135 is now "in the money" since we could sell the stock for $135 and then immediately buy it back at the market price of $132.

So the real value of this option is 135 - 132 = $3.

However, the current price of the option is $6.15.

Strike		Bid	Ask	□ Last
20d	Puts			
135		6.10	6.20	6.15
136		6.75	6.85	6.85
137		7.45	7.55	7.63
138		8.15	8.25	8.35
139		8.85	9.00	9.10

So the time value or Premium of this option is:

Market Price $6.15 - Real Value $3 = Time Value $3.15

And the same principle applies: This "Time Value" will decrease every day as we get closer to expiration until it is only a few cents on the day of expiration.

I like to say: "The Time Value is melting away like a snowman in Florida."

And that's a perfect example because at first, it melts away slowly, and then time decay accelerates and it melts away fast.

I made this illustration for you:

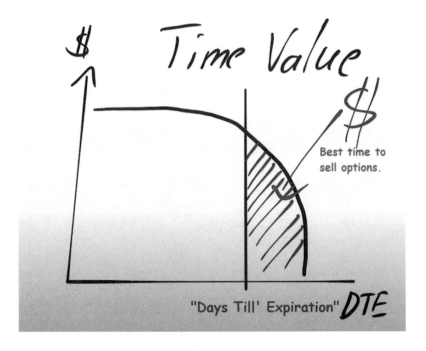

It's not fancy, but you get the idea:

As we get closer to expiration, the curved line shows how the Time Value decreases quite quickly.

And as option sellers, we want the time value to disappear quickly.

That's why we like to sell options with less than 14 days to expiration when trading The Wheel.

Theta - Your Best Friend When Trading The Wheel

Remember my "fancy" illustration in the previous chapter?

Theta is the measurement of Time Decay for an option contract, i.e. the slope of my hand-drawn curve.

Theta tells you how much the time decay decreases per day assuming everything else stays the same.

Let me show you an example.

The theta of the 135 Call with 55 days to expiration is 7.081 cents per day:

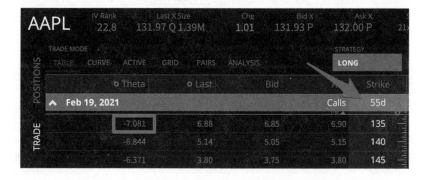

The theta of the 135 Call with 20 days to expiration is 9.675 cents per day:

Finally, the theta of the 135 Call with 5 days to expiration is 11.462 cents per day:

Here's a table that summarizes these 3 theta values:

Days to Expiration	Theta in cents / day
55	7.081
20	9.675
5	11.462

As you can see, the fewer days to expiration, the higher the "Theta".

When you are buying options, Time Decay can suck the life out of you. But when you are selling options, Time Decay is suddenly your best friend.

Much like life, there are no guarantees when it comes to trading...

...with the exception of Time Decay.

Time Decay is guaranteed to happen, as every day the Time Value of an option decreases.

And we are using THIS to our advantage when trading The Wheel.

Now you know what "Theta" is and why it is your best friend for The Wheel Strategy.

So let's take a look at finding the best stocks for The Wheel Strategy next.

Chapter 6

The Strategy - Part I: Finding The Right Stocks

Now that you have a solid foundation on how options work, we're now ready to start putting The Wheel strategy together.

The first, and probably the most important part is knowing what stocks and ETFs to use for this strategy... or more importantly, which stocks NOT to trade with The Wheel.

5 Steps To Finding The Right Stocks

Knowing how to pick the right stocks is absolutely key for this strategy.

With The Wheel, we're looking for quality companies.

And when it comes to finding the right stocks, most new traders don't know how to start, or where to begin looking.

I'm going to help make this process of finding the right stocks much easier for you.

I'll show you a step-by-step process how to find the best stocks and options to trade:

1. Find Stocks with No Earnings Before Expiration.

2. Find Stocks with High Volatility.

3. Find Stocks in an Uptrend or moving sideways with strong Support.

4. Check The Wheel Calculator.

5. Place the Trade.

Step 1: No Earnings Before Expiration

Earnings can turn a stock into quite the wild card.

Take a look at the chart below.

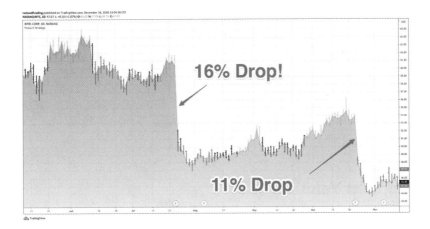

This is Intel (INTC) - one of the most predictable companies.

Usually, INTC trades in a small 1-2% range. But during the past 2 earnings reports, the moves have been crazy:

First, INTC lost 16% in a single day, and just a few months later - as the stock almost recovered these losses - INTC released the next earnings report and dropped 11%!

These are the moves that can cause you big losses when trading The Wheel.

Avoid these at all cost! Don't enter a trade if earnings will be released before the option that you sold expires.

Step 2: Find Stocks With High Implied Volatility (IV)

The next step is finding stocks with high implied volatility (IV).

This is important because Part I of The Wheel Strategy is selling Puts to collect Premium, and high IV means there will be higher Premiums. And I like to look for trades that give me a nice amount of Premium that I can collect each day.

So let's dive into Implied Volatility and how to find stocks with high IV.

Implied Volatility (IV)

Implied Volatility (IV), referred to as volatility or vol for short, is a representation of how volatile the underlying asset is expected to be before the expiration of the option.

Implied Volatility can be a good measure to determine if options are expensive or cheap.

An option with high IV would imply that there's a large move expected - but we don't know in which direction. Higher IV translates to more premium or extrinsic value in the contract.

A good example of options that will likely have higher IV, are options on a company that is going to announce earnings. Often traders are expecting a big move, but the direction of the move is uncertain. So options will be priced higher to reflect this uncertainty, which can be quantified as IV.

Another example is the outcome of a clinical trial for a pharmaceutical stock. Once the results are released, it can be good news or bad news. It's almost certain that this stock will make a big move, but we don't know the direction of the move yet.

So how can you find these stocks? - There are 3 ways to do it.

Tool #1: BarChart.com Screener

A great tool that you can use is the website www.barchart. com.

BarCharts is free to use and provides a scanner to search for stocks based on customizable filters.

In the following, I will show you a simple filter that you can use to find stocks with high implied volatility which can be great candidates for "The Wheel".

1. Go to https://barchart.com

2. Click on OPTIONS, which brings up the "options screener"

3. Click on SET FILTERS

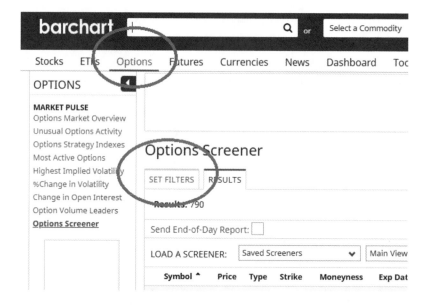

3. Select the following filters:

- **Earnings Date:** As explained in a previous chapter, it's important to make sure that we are not trading into earnings. Therefore, set the dates for the time frame you are looking for stocks to avoid stocks with earnings.

- **Exchange:** I'm fine searching through all of the listed exchanges, so I check all these boxes (AMEX, NYSE, and NASDAQ).

- **Strike Implied Volatility:** For here, I like to adjust the range between 30-50%. When it is above 50% the volatility is too high, and you have the danger of having a stock that is whip-sawing up and down. When it is below 30% premiums are usually too low.

- **Days To Expiration:** I set this at 7-21 days.

- **Last Trade Time:** Two dropdown boxes here. I set the first one to "made within last" and set the second one to "2 sessions."

- **Security Type:** I only check the box for "Stocks" and leave "ETF" and "Index" unchecked.

- **Option Type:** I only check the box for "Put" here and leave "Call" unchecked.

- **Volume:** I leave this at 0.

- **Open Interest:** I also leave this at 0.

- **Stock Price:** I set this to find stocks trading between $30-$250.

After you set the filters click the button at the bottom that says "SEE RESULTS."

The next page it brings you to will be all Put Options that match the criteria of the filters you just set.

If you look at your list of stocks from your refined search on BarCharts, there is a link titled "flipcharts" and it will give you a chart view of the first 10 charts on the list, which are also the highest-ranking, according to the criteria you set. You will easily be able to click from one chart to the next to see if the stock is trending in the direction you need it to.

Tool #2: TradingView Screener

Another tool you can use to find stocks with high IV is TradingView. TradingView is currently my favorite charting platform. It's entirely web based, and in my opinion has the best charting tools out there.

Once you've opened TradingView, at the top of the window you'll see an area where you can enter a ticker symbol.

For this example, we'll take a look at AAPL. I'll walk you through step-by-step how you can set up their stock screener to find stocks for The Wheel.

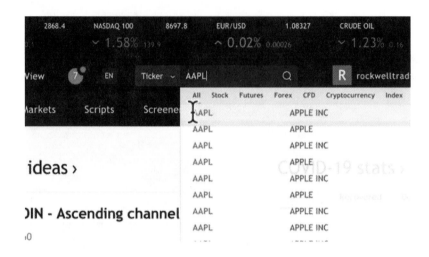

1. **Click on "Full Featured Charts"**

   Once you pick AAPL after typing it in the search bar, you want to click on the "Full-featured chart" button located at the top right of the chart.

Technicals

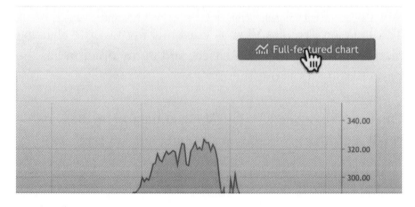

Once you click it, you will see a full-featured chart. You will have a chart on the top half, you will see "Stock Screener" & "Text Notes" at the bottom.

2. **Stock Screener:**

   Start by clicking on that "Stock Screener" tab that is on the lower left, it brings up the stock screener, and you will see predefined screeners in a dropdown menu, such as the Volume Gainers, Percent Change Gainers, and Percent Change Losers.

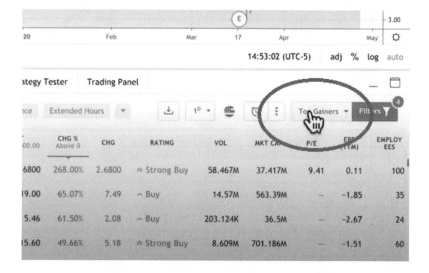

3. **Choose Predefined List:**

   To configure your own personalized scanner, just pick any one of them from the dropdown menu, it doesn't matter which, and I will show you how to configure it to find stocks to sell Put Options.

4. Adjusting Filters:

Once you pick any one of the predefined lists from the dropdown menu, right next to it, click on "Filters."

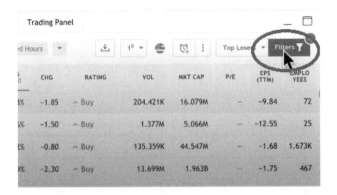

Now you can adjust the criteria like we did on BarCharts to find good stocks for The Wheel. Here are the four filters I like to adjust:

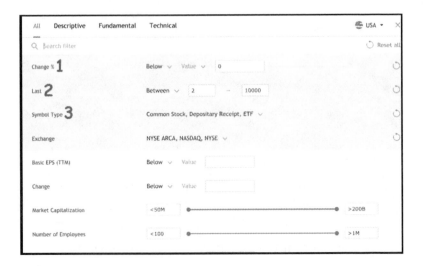

1. **Change %:** The first criteria you can alter is "change %." I like to see a percent daily change, where a stock has dropped more than 2%, so you enter a "-2" in this field. **Last:** The second criteria you can alter is the "Last," or last price. I like to find stocks that are trading between $30-$250. This is the price range I personally like to use, but you can set this dollar range to your personal preference.

2. **Symbol Type:** In terms of "Symbol Type" which is the third field that I change, I'm only looking at common stock, so I check the box for "Common Stock" and leave the rest unchecked.

3. **Volume:** The fourth and final criterion I change is the "Volume" filter. I adjust this filter for stocks that are trading at, at least, one million shares per day, up to ANY. I just leave it at the max. These are the only four things that I am changing. You do not need to alter any other fields in this Stock Screener.

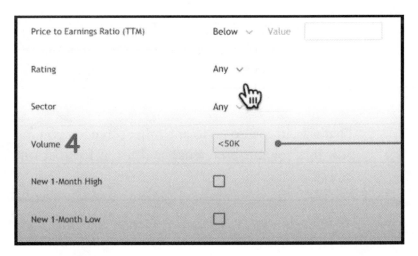

4. **Saving Your Settings:**
   After making these four changes, click the "X" at the top right of this "Filters" window, and you will see a list of the stocks that meet the criteria in the dropdown menu. The predefined screener you altered now has an asterisk next to its name, signifying that you have made changes to it. Click on this dropdown menu again, and you will see "Save Screens As..." at the very top. You can name this new custom Stock Screener anything you want.

5. **Customizing Columns:**
   You will now see the stocks that meet these new criteria in the results, and you can simplify this even more. There are multiple columns of information such as the Ticker, Last, Change %, and many others.

   I personally don't need most of these columns, and you can remove a column by right-clicking the name, and selecting the "Remove column."

   I only like to keep Ticker, Last, Change %, and Sector. These are the only four columns I'm interested in. You can also save these column preferences just like we saved our filter preferences.

   That way, if you do go to any other screener, you can pick this column preference and use it for that one as well.

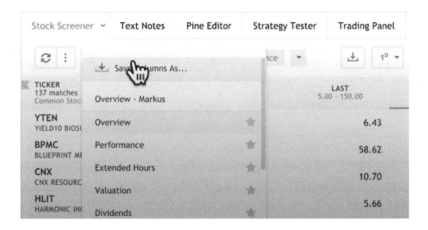

You save it by clicking the dropdown menu right above the stock list and selecting "Save Columns As…" and naming it whatever you want.

Tool #3: PowerX Optimizer

The tools above are free, and they have their limitations:

As you can see, they are not very easy to set up.

And you will notice that the results are "ok." These tools do the best they can with their limited functionality.

I personally use **The PowerX Optimizer.**

It's a tool that I developed specifically for "The PowerX Strategy" and "The Wheel Strategy."

The Power Optimizer shows me the best stocks to trade and the probabilities of success.

If you are interested in learning more about this tool, then check out myTradingRoutine.com.

On that website, you will find a video in which I show you step by step how I use this tool every day to trade.

Now that we've gone through a few examples of different Stock Screeners and how I have them set up, let's now discuss how to find and draw key support and resistance levels on the charts.

Step 3: Find Stocks In An Uptrend or Strong Support

When finding the right stock, make sure that it is either trending upwards or trending sideways at a strong support level. Stocks that are trending this way are ideal for The Wheel Strategy.

The key question: How exactly do you figure out if a stock has strong support?

As a trader, you must be able to identify strong support and resistance. From my experience, a lot of traders tend to over complicate the process of identifying these levels. So in this next section, I'll show you how I quickly and easily determine key support and resistance levels.

Support And Resistance

So what exactly are support and resistance levels? These are levels that the price of a stock, ETF, etc. has trouble moving through. A stock may pause at support and resistance or even bounce off it.

Support is the level below the price acting as a floor that the price has trouble moving below.

Resistance is the level above the price acting as a ceiling that the price has trouble moving above. When the price does break through a resistance level, that level often becomes support. And the opposite is true. When price breaks through a support level, that level often becomes its new resistance line.

There are two types of support and resistance:

1. Static - On a chart, it can be a straight line or be at an angle. Examples are Fibonacci levels or simple trend lines.

2. Dynamic - These are types of support and resistance lines that adjust automatically. Examples are moving averages or Bollinger Bands.

Using Tradingview To Find Support And Resistance

For all of my charting, I prefer to use TradingView.

Of course, you can also use your broker's platform like ThinkOrSwim by TD Ameritrade or Street Smart Edge by Charles Schwab.

If you'd like to check out TradingView, I'm using the "Pro" version: https://www.rockwelltrading.com/tradingview

You can add support and resistance levels on the chart yourself as a visual reference.

To get started, you can type in any stock ticker in the search bar.

In the following I will use TSLA as an example to show you how to do it.

Finding Static Support & Resistance Levels

Now let's take a look at how we can find stocks with an overall uptrend or strong support using TradingView.

If you are using another charting platform, these steps will be very similar.

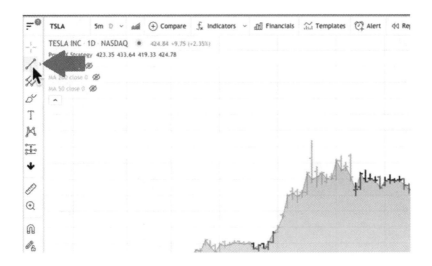

To add a line to the chart, in this case, to illustrate static support and resistance lines, click on the line tool icon from the column to the left of the chart.

To use it to draw your trendline, just click/hold the left mouse button on the chart where you want the line to start, and drag the mouse to where you want the line to end, and unclick.

Support lines can either be at an angle or horizontal.

To find a support line, you want to find points on the chart where prices dipped and draw a line connecting them. These dips will act as touchpoints and you want to connect as many touchpoints as possible.

This line represents a support level where prices are bouncing. The support level acts as a barrier and the price has trouble breaking below.

As you can see on this TSLA chart, whenever the price would drop, it would not drop past this support line.

This is a sign of strong support.

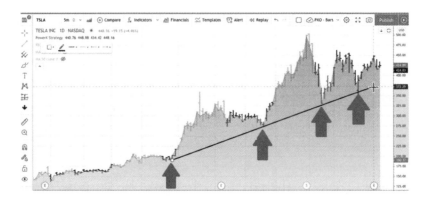

You find resistance the same way - only instead of drawing a line connecting dips in the chart, you draw a line connecting the spikes.

These spikes also act as touchpoints and you want to connect as many as possible.

This line is the level the price had trouble breaking through, acting as its resistance level.

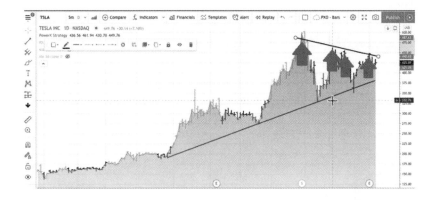

So how do you find strong static support and resistance?

- **Zoom out of the chart.**
  You can't look at too narrow of a timeframe to find strong support and resistance, sometimes you need to go out as far as several months. The further you zoom out, the stronger the support and resistance.

- **Focus on the 'big' support and resistance levels.**
  Don't worry about support and resistance on 5-minutes charts, unless you are day trading. Focus on support and resistance on daily and weekly charts.

- The more "touches" the stronger the support and resistance.

Here is an example of a stock, WYNN, that I recently traded.

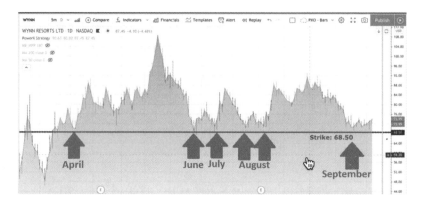

When I was looking at this stock, I saw support around $68.50-$69.

The prices touched and bounced off of this level several times: it happened in April, June, July, August, and September.

This seems like a strong support level because the support level held over a 5 month period.

If I would have been zoomed in too much, I would have only seen where the price touched the support line in September, maybe August, and it would have been difficult to recognize strong support.

Let's take a look at the resistance line for this same chart.

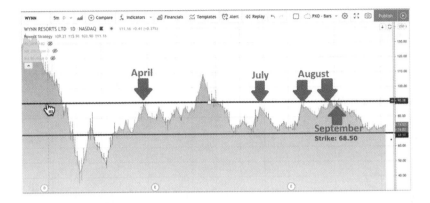

There was strong resistance at the $90 level. The price bounced off of this level in April, July, August, and September.

So as you can see, during this 5-month time frame, WYNN bounced back and forth between the $68.50 support and the $90 resistance levels.

I use the support level to determine what Strike Price to sell the Put at when I am trading with The Wheel Strategy.

If the chart is showing strong support, I will consider selling Put Options with strike prices at or below these support levels.

Finding Dynamic Support & Resistance Levels

"Dynamic support and resistance lines" is a fancy name for moving averages.

The most famous moving averages that most professional hedge fund managers use are 50, 100, and 200 day SMAs (simple moving averages). These are the most important dynamic support and resistance lines.

What makes them "dynamic?" Take a look at this chart of the NASDAQ:

On this chart, the red line represents the 50 day moving average, while the blue line represents the 200 day moving average.

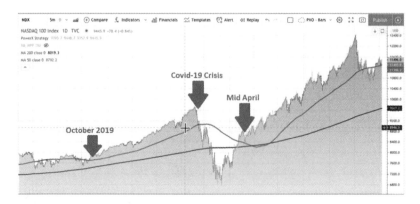

You can see that the 50 day moving average has acted as a support, starting in October of 2019.

You can then see a steep dip where the Covid-19 pandemic first hit, but by mid April, the 50 day moving average went back to acting as a support once again.

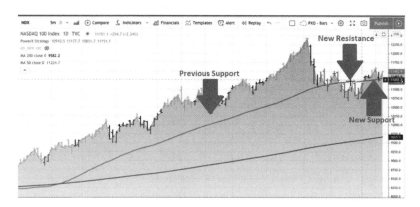

Whenever a price breaks through a moving average, the previous 50 moving average will become a new resistance.

And when the price breaks through this new resistance, it then becomes the new support level.

Note: The 200 day moving average is more important when looking at longer term trends.

Dynamic support lines do have their limitations, however.

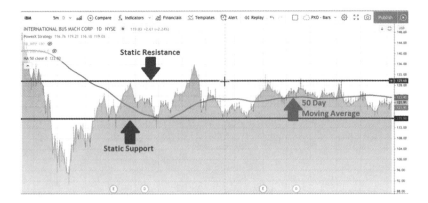

If you notice on this chart of IBM, the 50 day moving average doesn't really show any support and resistance.

But when you use static levels - as described in the previous chapter - it's rather easy to find support and resistance.

And often, static support and resistance levels are stronger than dynamic ones.

That's why I prefer plotting my own support and resistance lines as outlined in the previous chapter.

But if you're newer to technical analysis and would prefer a more automated solution, then there are a multitude of different indicators that will plot them for you.

Step 4: Check The Wheel Calculator

The secret to successful trading is being very picky and making sure that you are getting the very best trades.

I would NEVER place a Wheel trade without running it through my tool, "The Wheel Calculator."

Trading without the right tools is like trying to compete in Nascar riding on a llama. Nothing against the llama, but you wouldn't stand a chance.

When trading, you are trading against some of the smartest minds in the world. And if you want to compete and win, you need to be armed with the best tools to give yourself an edge. Trading without the right tools is like bringing a knife to a gunfight.

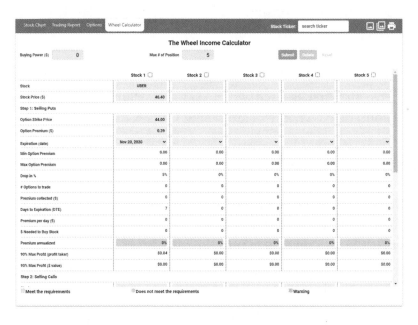

The Wheel Calculator is a tool that my Head Coach Mark Hodge and I developed, and it is now built into our proprietary trading software, **The PowerX Optimizer.**

It is designed to quickly show you whether an option meets the requirements that I'm looking for to trade The Wheel Strategy.

It is very easy to use, and it does all the calculations for you. This will save you not only time but money, as it will keep you from making costly mistakes.

All you need to do is enter the required information for the option, and The Wheel Calculator does the rest.

You simply start by inputting your buying power and the max number of positions that you want to take. I like to manage 5 positions at a time.

From there, The Wheel Calculator is broken down into two steps, the first is used when you are selling Puts, and the second helps when you are selling Calls.

Let's start with Selling Puts:

When you find a stock that you are interested in and you've figured out what price you would be willing to own it at, you enter the following data into the calculator:

- Stock Ticker
- Current Stock Price
- Option Strike Price
- Option Premium
- Expiration Date

The Wheel Calculator will crunch the numbers, and you will be able to decide if selling Puts at this Strike Price meets our requirements. You can then decide if the trade makes sense, if you should sell a different Strike Price based on the results, or just pass on this trade altogether.

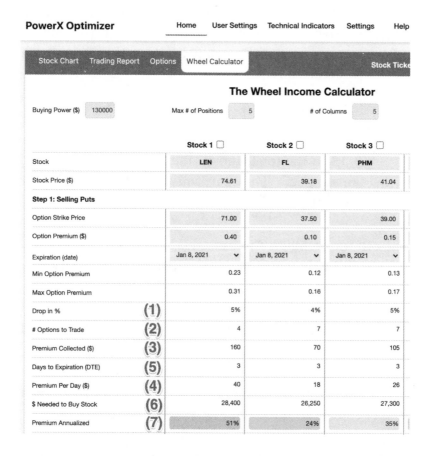

When looking at a Strike Price, The Wheel Calculator shows you exactly what percent a stock can drop in price (1) before the put goes "in the money" and possibly gets assigned.

The Wheel Calculator will clearly show you...

(2) How many Puts you can sell based on your buying power.

(3) How much Premium you will collect per contract.

(4) The Premium you will collect per day for each contract, making it easier to make sure you will be earning enough Premium Per Day (PPD), on each position.

(5) The number of days until expiration.

(6) And the total amount the shares will cost if you are assigned. This way you don't overextend your account.

The cell for Premium Annualized (7) in the spreadsheet will even be highlighted in either green, yellow, or red so it's easy to see how the collected premium stacks up.

- Green indicates that selling the Put Option would meet our requirements,

- Red means it would not, i.e. the premium is not high enough to trade, and

- Yellow indicates a warning that the premium is unusually high.

Premium Per Day ($)	40	18	26
$ Needed to Buy Stock	28,400	26,250	27,300
Premium Annualized	51%	24%	35%

When you see a yellow warning, it is often a sign that you overlooked something, e.g. trading into earnings or the strike price is too close.

A "warning" doesn't mean you shouldn't take the trade. It just means that you should double and triple check the trade to make sure you haven't overlooked anything.

The Wheel Calculator also helps when you have been assigned shares and are ready to start selling Calls against these shares.

I will cover selling Calls in Chapter 8, but when you get to the point when you are selling Calls, all you need to do is...

1.)   Input the stock ticker,

2.)   the price the stock was bought at,

3.)   the number of shares you own,

4.)   the Call Option strike price,

5.)   Premium you would collect per share and

6.)   the expiration date of the Call Option.

Stock 1 ☐

Step 2: Selling Calls

Stock	**(1)**	**LEN**
Price Stock was Bought At	**(2)**	71.00
# of Shares	**(3)**	400
Option Strike Price	**(4)**	73.00
Option Premium ($)	**(5)**	0.80
Expiration (date)	**(6)**	Jan 15, 2021 ˅

The calculator will show you…

7.) What percentage the price of the stock would have to move to get to the Strike Price,

8.) the number of options being traded,

9.) the total amount of Premium being collected,

10.) The days until expiration (DTE),

11.) how much Premium is being collected per day,

12.) position value,

13.) and the option Premium annualized.

Rise in %	**(7)**	3%
# Options to Trade	**(8)**	4
Premium Collected ($)	**(9)**	320
Days to Expiration (DTE)	**(10)**	10
Premium Per Day ($)	**(11)**	29
Position Value	**(12)**	28,400
Option Premium annualized	**(13)**	37%

If the stock is exercised, it will also show you...

14.) What the profit would be from selling those shares,

15.) the percentage of stock gains for the holding period,

16.) and the total gain from both the stock and option.

Here's what it looks like in the Wheel Calculator:

Stock Gains If Exercised	**(14)**	800.00
Stock Gains for Holding Period	**(15)**	3%
Total Gain (Option and Stock)	**(16)**	**$1,120.00**

You can already see how The Wheel Calculator is such an invaluable tool. By doing the math for us and presenting the information to us in an organized manner, we save time, prevent costly errors, and maybe a few headaches.

OK, so now that you know how to find a stock that meets our criteria after being run through our "Wheel Calculator," now it's time to actually place the trade.

In the next 3 chapters, I will review these three steps in the Wheel in more detail:

1. Selling Puts,

2. Assignment, and

3. Selling Calls

Chapter 7

The Strategy - Part II: Selling Puts

There are two more things I need to address before you can start trading "The Wheel Strategy."

Capital Requirements

When trading The Wheel Strategy, it is possible (and often desirable) to get "assigned" shares when a stock closes below the Put strike price that you've sold.

We will talk about assignment in more detail in the next chapter, but it is important to touch on it now.

As explained in the previous chapter, before you start selling Puts, you must first pick a stock that you are 100% comfortable owning at the strike price that you've sold.

And that's why you need to have enough buying power in your account in case you are assigned.

The amount you need depends on your personal goals, but as a general guideline, I recommend that you have at least $20,000 of buying power in your trading account for this strategy.

If you use a margin account, this means that you need to put $10,000 in cash into the account.

Cash Secured vs Naked Puts

Step 1 of The Wheel Strategy is "Selling Puts."

And there's 2 ways to sell puts: cash secured or naked.

Here's what this means:

Let's say you want to sell puts on Lennar (LEN) with a strike price of 71:

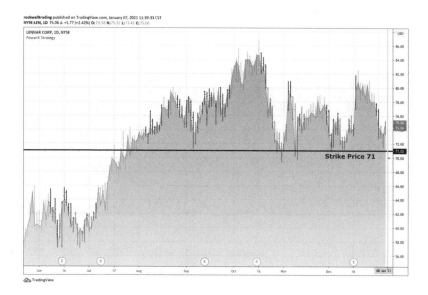

rockwelltrading published on TradingView.com, January 07, 2021 11:39:33 CST
NYSE:LEN, 1D 75.06 ▲ +1.77 (+2.42%) O: 73.58 H: 75.32 L: 73.41 C: 75.06

LENNAR CORP, 1D, NYSE
PowerX Strategy

Strike Price 71

TradingView

If LEN is trading below \$71 on expiration date, you are getting assigned, and you have to buy 100 shares of LEN for each option that you sold at \$71.

If you sold 1 option, you would have to buy 100 shares at \$71, therefore you need \$7,100 in your account to do this.

Let's say you have \$10,000 in your trading account.

When the trade is "cash secured" this means that your broker requires the full amount of \$7,100 that would be required to buy 100 shares at the strike price sold (\$71).

But here's the kicker:

Most brokers don't require the full \$7,100 for selling the put.

Tastyworks, the broker that I am using, only requires $1,050.25!

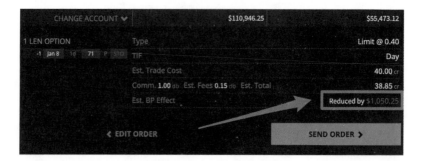

This means that you *could* actually sell 9 Put options. For these 9 options, the broker would require $9,452.25.

And since you have $10,000 in your trading account, you could collect 9x the premium, right?

WRONG!

Because if you would get assigned, you need $7,100 for each option that you sold, i.e. $7,100 * 9 = $63,900.

And since you don't have enough money in your account, you would get a dreaded "margin call" from your broker for over $53,900!

A Margin Call occurs when you don't have enough money in your account to satisfy the account requirements set by your broker. It means that your broker will require that you wire the money, in this case $53,900. And usually you have to do it the same day.

If you don't wire the money, your broker will sell the shares the next day for whatever price he can get. And this means that you lose control over this trade!

So you're caught "with your pants down", and that's why they're called "naked puts."

When you sell a naked put you are only putting a fraction of the trade value up as collateral. But you can get into trouble when you are assigned this way. So I always like to base my trades on my stock buying power instead.

So why would the broker let you sell these Puts and require only $1,050.25 when the shares would cost $7,100?

He does this for two reasons.

- Reason number 1: Most options expire worthless.

- Reason number 2: Even if they don't expire worthless, most traders buy the option back, so they close it before it expires. And the broker knows that.

- This is why they often only require 15% - $20% of the full margin. And that's ok if you plan to close the trade before expiration.

However, when trading The Wheel, you actually want to get assigned. It is a part of the strategy!

Remember, if we don't get assigned, we collect the Premium. If we do get assigned, we then sell Calls against our shares and collect even MORE Premium.

So when trading The Wheel, always make sure you have enough to cover the full cash value of the position and never rely solely on "naked Puts"!

Selling Puts On LEN

Now that you understand the difference between Cash Secured Puts and Naked Puts and why I think Cash Secured is the only way to go, let's look at an actual example.

In this example, I was trading options on Lennar (LEN):

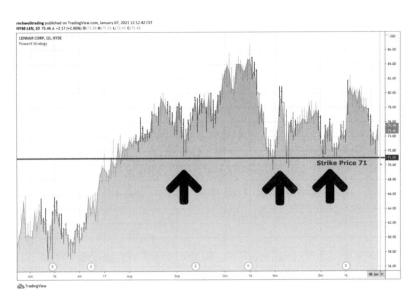

I saw strong support at 71 on the chart. This support level was touched several times, and it held every single time.

So I decided to sell Puts with a 71 strike price.

I was able to get $0.42 per option with 4 days to expiration, and I sold 4 Puts.

For these 4 puts, I received $42 * 4 = $168 in Premium.

A few days later, on expiration day, LEN closed above $71, and I was able to keep the whole premium of $168.

Now this trade is closed, and the broker is releasing the margin so that I can take the next trade.

That was easy!

But let me show you another example of a trade where I got assigned.

Selling Puts on UBER - and getting assigned

In Summer 2020, I noticed that UBER has shown some support at the 30 level:

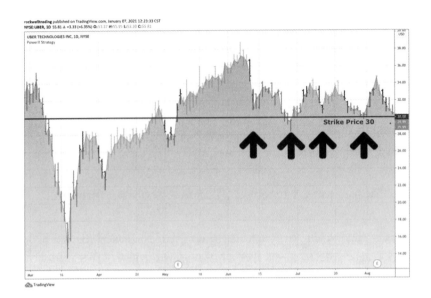

So on August 7, I sold Puts with a strike price of 30.

They would expire on August 14th, so I had only 7 days until expiration.

I could get $0.25 in premium for each option, and I decided to sell 7 puts. So the total Premium that I received was $175.

If UBER would close above 30 on August 14th (expiration day), then I would simply keep the $175 that I collected and move on to the next trade.

But UBER had different plans: On August 14th, UBER closed at 29.99, and I got assigned. Now I was the proud owner of 700 UBER shares.

Chapter 8

The Strategy - Part III: Selling Calls

When you pick the right stocks and the right strike prices, you won't be assigned often.

But you shouldn't be afraid of getting assigned, because it's part of The Wheel strategy. Getting assigned gets the Wheel "rolling."

In this chapter, you will learn what to do after getting assigned shares of stock.

Covered vs Naked Calls

When you sell a Call Option without owning 100 shares of stock per option, then you are selling a Naked Call.

If you do own the underlying security, then you are selling a Call that is covered by shares that you own, known as a Covered Call.

Since getting assigned is part of the Wheel Strategy, there will be times when you are buying shares at the strike price of the put that you sold. And when you take possession of these shares, the next step in "The Wheel" is to sell Covered Calls.

Selling Covered Calls works great with The Wheel Strategy because they allow you to collect more premium on the stocks that you have in your account.

You will sell 1 Call for every 100 shares that you have in your portfolio.

And even though it might be scary to get assigned, it can be the most lucrative part of the strategy.

The most important thing to remember is that you only sell 1 call per 100 shares that are assigned, because otherwise, you're selling naked calls.

And selling naked calls is a super risky strategy since the risk is unlimited.

Let me explain:

When you sell a PUT, you have to buy the stock at the underlying strike price.

In our UBER example from the previous chapter, we sold puts with a strike price of 30. This means that we have to buy 100 shares per put option that we sold.

So the capital requirement for this trade is $30 * 100 = $3,000.

And this is also your maximum risk, since the stock can't go below 0.

On the other hand, when you sell a CALL, you are obligated to sell 100 shares for each call at the strike price sold.

Let's say that you sold a call with a strike price of $30.

So you have to sell 100 shares of UBER at $30.

If UBER moves up to $40, you would lose $10 * 100 shares = $1,000.

And if UBER moves up to $60, you would lose $30 * 100 shares = $3,000.

If UBER moves up to $150, you would lose $120 * 100 shares = $12,000.

There's no limit how high UBER can go, and therefore your risk is unlimited.

Always keep in mind:

- When selling NAKED PUTS, your risk is limited to the strike price * 100.

- When selling NAKED CALLS, your risk is unlimited!

Therefore, make sure that you only sell COVERED CALLS, because then you technically have NO RISK with the option.

Getting Assigned Is Good!

Many traders who are new to trading The Wheel try to avoid assignment.

And I understand why:

When you are getting assigned, you will usually see a LOSS in your account.

Here's an example:

If we sold the UBER 30 PUT, we would get assigned when UBER is below $30 on the day of the option expiration.

Let's say UBER is trading at $29 on expiration day.

This means that you have to buy shares at $30, and they are now only worth $29.

So you have an "unrealized loss" of $1 per share, i.e. $100 per option that you sold since options came in "100-packs" - as you already know.

And if you sold 7 puts, then you would see a $700 unrealized loss.

That might scare you!

The important thing:

It's an unrealized loss.

You would only realize the loss if you would sell your shares right now.

But that's not what we will do.

Our plan is to keep the shares, sell calls against them and collect more Premium.

UBER Trade Continued

Let's revisit the UBER trade that we started back in Chapter 7.

To recap:

1. I saw that UBER was going sideways and had support at the $30 level.

2. I decided that I'm comfortable owning UBER shares for $30 IF I would get assigned.

3. I sold 7 Put Options for UBER at the 30 Strike Price, with one week until expiration for $25 per contract.

4. I collected $175 in total for the 7 contracts ($25 for each contract) in one week.

5. On expiration day, the price of UBER dipped below $30 and I was assigned these shares.

6. 7 Put Options at 100 shares each means I had to buy 700 shares of UBER at $30 per share.

7. 700 shares of UBER at $30 each means I paid $21,000 in total for this trade.

So this was Part I and Part II of The Wheel: Selling Puts and Assignment.

Now Part III is selling Covered Calls against the shares of UBER I was just assigned, and this is what we'll review now.

Since I had 700 shares of UBER I sold 7 Covered Calls against these shares.

I sold 7 Calls with a Strike Price of 31 for $0.52, or $52 for each contract, for a total of $364.

These Calls had an expiration date of August 28th, and I made this trade on August 21st.

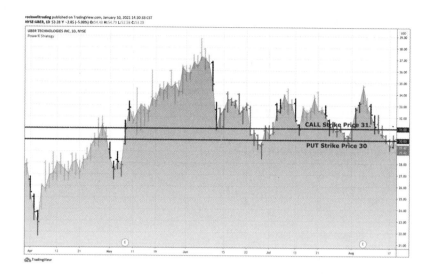

Here are three possible scenarios on how this trade could have ended up at expiration on August 28th:

Scenario 1:

The price of UBER closes above the assigned price but below the Call Strike of 31

Let's recap:

- We sold puts and collected $175 in premium

- We got assigned 700 shares

- We sold calls and collected $364 in premium

If UBER closes above the assigned price, we will keep the premium of the options that we sold = $175 (put sold) + $364 (call sold) = $539.

PLUS, we will make money on the stocks that we own.

As an example, if UBER closes at $30.50 on the expiration date of August 28th, we make $0.50 per share. Since we own 700 shares, we would make an additional $350 on the shares.

So our total profit would be:

- $175 from selling puts

- $364 from selling calls

- $350 from the shares that we owned

- **$889 total profit**

At this point, our calls expire worthless. We don't have any open option positions, and we have 2 possibilities:

- We can now choose to close the trade for a profit and start The Wheel again or

- We can sell more calls against our existing position and get more premium.

Scenario 2:
The price of UBER closes above the Call Strike of 31

Let's say that UBER closes at $32 on August 28th (expiration day).

In this case, we would still keep our premium from selling the puts and call, but our profit from the stock is limited to $1 per share.

Here's why: We bought the shares at $30 and have to sell them at $31, since we sold a call at a strike price of 31.

We bought 700 shares at 30 and sold them at 31, so we make $700.

So our total profit would be:

- $175 from selling puts

- $364 from selling calls

- <u>$700 profits from the shares that we owned</u>

- **$1,239 total profit**

At this point, the calls we sold are "in the money" and the call buyer has the right to buy shares from us at the 31 strike that we sold.

So our shares are "called away".

The shares that we bought for $30 are taken out of our account to fulfill our obligation to the call buyer. At this point, we no longer have a position in UBER and our account shows the profit breakdown shown above. This is what traders call "being flat".

The trade is closed and we can now look for other opportunities.

Scenario 3:
The price of UBER closes below the assigned price of 30

Let's say that UBER closes at $29 on August 28th (expiration day).

In this case, we would still keep our premium from selling the put and call, but we don't make any money on the shares.

In fact, we now show an unrealized loss of $1 per share since we bought the shares at $30 and the current price is $29. So our P&L will show an unrealized loss of $700.

In summary, we see:

- $175 in profits from selling puts

- $364 in profits from from selling calls

- $700 unrealized loss since our shares are "under water"

- **$539 in realized profits and $700 in unrealized profits**

The good news:

The calls that we sold expired worthless and we can now sell more calls against our existing 700 shares - and collect more premium.

The Wheel is turning...

Of course, at some point, if the price of the stock keeps dropping, we might not be able to sell calls anymore. And we will talk about this scenario in the next chapter.

But THIS is how The Wheel Strategy works:

You just follow the same steps over and over, and "The Wheel" just keeps on turning.

In case you're wondering what happened to me in this trade:

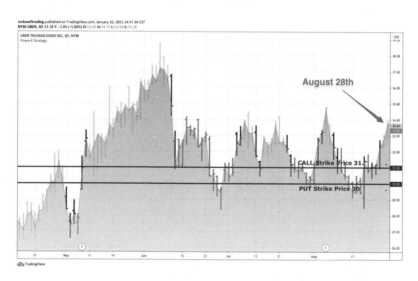

On August 28th, UBER closed at $33.63 (Scenario 2).

So my total profit on this trade was:

- $175 from selling puts

- $364 from selling calls

- <u>$700 unrealized profits from the shares that we owned</u>

- **$1,239 total profit**

I entered the trade on August 7th.

I exited the trade 21 days later on August 28th.

I made $1,239 in 21 days = $59 per day.

If I can repeat this over and over, I would make $59 * 360 days = $21,240 per year.

And I only needed $21,000 for this trade, so that would be **101%** annual return on investment (ROI). Not bad at all...

Chapter **9**

What You Need To Know Before Trading This Strategy

Now you know the details of The Wheel Strategy, and there are a few other things I would like to 'arm' you with before getting started.

Options Trading Permissions

Before you can place a trade, you first must have the right options trading permissions.

There are four levels of options trading:

- Level 1: Selling Cash Secured Puts and Covered Calls

- Level 2: Level 1 + Buying Options

- Level 3: Level 1+ 2 + Debit and Credit Spreads

- Level 4: Level 1+ 2 + 3 + Advanced Options Strategies

If you want to trade The Wheel, you need just the basic Level 1 options permissions.

But you typically need to tell your broker what type of options you want to trade when opening an account.

If you don't specify anything, the broker will assign you "Level 0", i.e no permissions.

Below is a sample account opening form from TD Ameritrade, in which they ask "what type of activity do you plan to conduct in your trading account?"

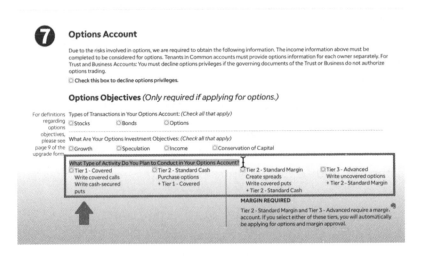

It doesn't matter whether you have a cash account or a retirement account:

All you need for trading The Wheel Strategy is the lowest permissions possible.

On this form pictured above, this would be Tier I.

If you already have an account and don't know what trading permissions you have, contact your broker and tell him to adjust your trading permissions so that you can "sell cash secured puts and covered calls."

You shouldn't have any problems getting the needed permissions.

Testing The Strategy

If you are brand new to trading and haven't yet used a paper trading simulator, you should.

Some traders won't use a paper trading simulator when they are first getting started because they don't feel like it's an accurate representation of the real markets.

And to an extent, that's true. Without risking real money, you're not going to experience the emotions that come along with risk just trading in a simulator. But even with that said, I'm still a huge fan of trading simulators.

Think about it: How do they train pilots?

Every pilot has to start on a simulator. Then, after many hours on a simulator, and after passing a series of tests, a pilot is finally able to get behind the controls of a real plane.

If they never had this time on a simulator, would it make sense for them to start out in a real plane and start flying?

Of course not!

Even though trading on a simulator isn't exactly the same as trading with real money, you should take trading on a simulator seriously - for a very simple reason:

If you lose "money" on a simulator, you are almost guaranteed to lose money in real trading.

Think about the example of training pilots:

Do you think if an aspiring pilot crashed in the simulator every single time they would say, *"Ah, don't worry about it, you'll figure it out once you're up in the air! Just get in the plane, you're going to do great!"*

Of course not!

And it is the same idea with a trading simulator:

Trade on a simulator until you are seeing some consistency. Being successful on a simulator doesn't guarantee you will be successful when you are trading live. But if you are not successful using a simulator, chances are you will not be successful when trading live.

I recommend trading on a simulator for at least 40 trades.

40 trades give you enough data to have a statistically significant sample. Everything less will distort the result. Think about it: You could place only 3 trades on a simulator, and even though all of them are winning trades, it doesn't mean that you will have a 100% winning percentage.

Even 10-20 trades aren't enough. Take the time on the simulator and go through 40 trades. Your trading account will thank you!

So where do you find a trading simulator?

There are several companies out there that offer simulators, and I've tested over a dozen of them. Most of them were not very realistic. However, the one that I did find to be the most realistic is "paperMoney" by ThinkorSwim.

It is offered through TD Ameritrade's ThinkorSwim platform. You don't need a real trading account with them to use it. All you have to do is sign up by giving them some basic personal information, such as your name, email, and address.

Something to keep in mind before you start paper trading:

Most simulators have a button that says "Reset All" or something similar. This allows you to wipe out whatever you did and start fresh.

This can sound very appealing when you first start paper trading. You take some bad trades in the beginning and decide you want to just start over.

DO NOT do this!

In real life, there is no such button when live trading with real money.

It would be nice if such a button existed when live trading, and you could just push it after a bad trade and all the money was put back in your account.

But since you can't do this in live trading, you shouldn't use this feature while paper trading.

Take your paper trading seriously, and treat it like you would live trading.

You want to make sure that you learn how to climb out of a hole after a few losing trades.

You will make mistakes with paper trading just like you would with live trading, and it's better to make these mistakes on a simulator than losing your hard earned money.

The important thing: You have to LEARN from your mistakes and make sure that you don't repeat them - especially not when you're trading with real money.

So even if you already have trading experience, I highly recommend 'cutting your teeth' on a simulator to get more confident trading something new, like The Wheel.

Chapter 10

What To Do When The Market Crashes

One of the most frequently asked question around this strategy is this:

"What do you do when you sold a put and the market is crashing?"

In this chapter, we will talk about this in detail.

When selling put options, there is the possibility of being assigned. And this is where it can get risky if you don't know what you are doing.

So what exactly is assignment - especially when selling puts?

Assignment means that the seller of the options contract (YOU) has the obligation to fulfill the contract by BUYING the stock at the Strike Price of the options contract at expiration - if the buyer of the Options contract decides to exercise it.

And the buyer will exercise the right to SELL the stock at the strike price if the stock closes BELOW the strike price at expiration.

Here's an example:

Let's say you sold the UBER Put with a strike price of 30.

This means that the buyer of this put option can force you to BUY 100 shares of UBER at $30. So he would SELL 100 shares of UBER at $30.

And if the stock is trading at a lower price, let's say $29, then he can BUY 100 shares of UBER in the market for $29 and sell it to you for $30. So he would make $1 profit per share = $100.

Therefore, it's almost certain that the buyer of the put option that you sell will exercise it if the stock price is below the strike price on expiration day.

As you know, getting assigned shares is part of The Wheel, because now you can sell calls against the shares you own (see Chapter 8).

There's only one problem:

If a stock moves sharply lower, you might have a large unrealized loss. And you might not be able to get any premium when trying to sell calls.

Here's an example:

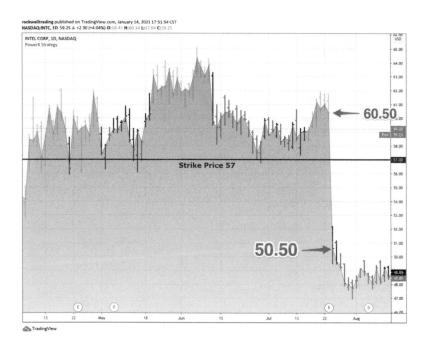

Intel (INTC) was trading in a nice range between 57 and 63.

There was solid support at 57, and you might have been tempted to sell a put at the 57 level.

(Let's just assume for a moment that you completely forgot about the rule "Don't trade into Earnings!")

The day before INTC reported earnings, the stock closed at 60.50.

And the next day, the stock moved massively lower and closed at 50.50.

In this case, you could have been forced to BUY 100 shares of INTC at 57.

And now they are only worth 50.50, so you are losing $6.50 per share. That's $650 for each 100 shares that you own!

Since the stock moved sharply lower, you won't get any premium for calls with strike prices of 57 and above.

So you are caught with your pants down.

What do you do now?

These things can happen when you trade The Wheel strategy, and in the next few minutes, I will show you how to "rescue" a trade like this.

Managing A Losing Trade

Yes, it happened to me:

I sold a put on TQQQ at a strike price of 150 right before this stock crashed 39%!

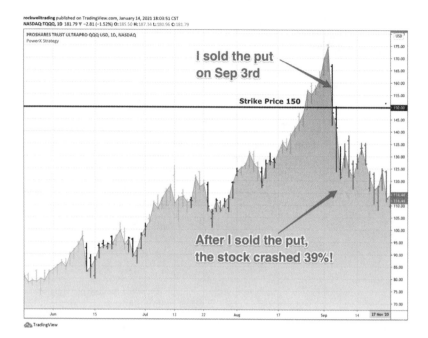

rockwelltrading published on TradingView.com, January 14, 2021 18:03:51 CST
NASDAQ:TQQQ, 1D 181.79 ▼ −2.81 (−1.52%) O: 185.50 H: 187.34 L: 180.96 C: 181.79

PROSHARES TRUST ULTRAPRO QQQ USD, 1D, NASDAQ
PowerX Strategy

I sold the put
on Sep 3rd

Strike Price 150

After I sold the put,
the stock crashed 39%!

To understand how to manage a losing trade, I will walk you through every single transaction that I did to turn this trade around: from a $4,000 loss to a $2,500 profit!

Let's get started.

On September 3rd, I sold 1 TQQQ Put expiring on Sep 4th with a strike price of 150. I collected $0.66 in premium, i.e. $66.

On September 4th, TQQQ closed at 141.64, and I received 100 shares of TQQQ at a price of 150.

On September 8th, TQQQ closed at 121.44, and I am down $2,856. Ouch!

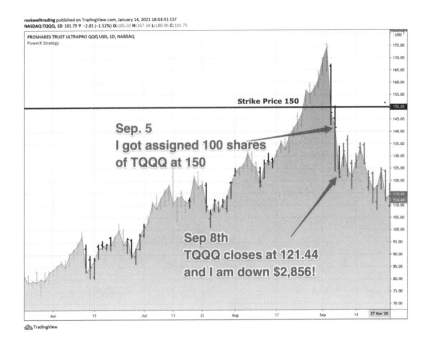

The "good news":

I received $66 in premium when I sold the Put, and I can keep this premium no matter what. Therefore my "cost basis" of the TQQQ shares is $150 - $0.66 = $149.34.

So I am "only" losing $2,856 - $66 = $2,790. □

Moving on…

On September 10th, TQQQ moved a little bit higher, and I was able to sell the 150 Call expiring on September 18 for $2.10.

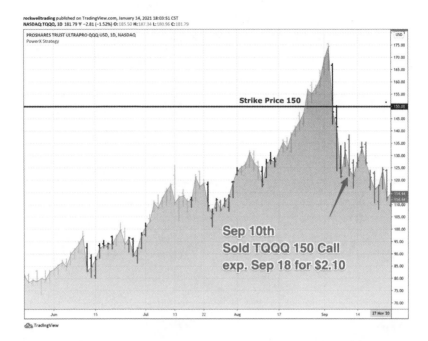

rockwelltrading published on TradingView.com, January 14, 2021 18:03:51 CST
NASDAQ:TQQQ, 1D 181.79 ▼ -2.81 (-1.52%) O: 185.50 H: 187.34 L: 180.96 C: 181.79

Just one day later, on September 11th, I was able to buy this call back for $0.37, so I made 2.10 - 0.37 = 1.73.

So I was able to reduce my cost basis for the stock by another 1.73.

Since I can keep the premium of the options I sold no matter what the stock does, my cost basis is now 147.61.

As long as TQQQ stays below 147.61, I'm losing money.

But if TQQQ would move above 147.61, I would start making money.

On September 15th, TQQQ moved a little bit higher, and I was able to sell another 150 Call expiring September 18th for $0.45.

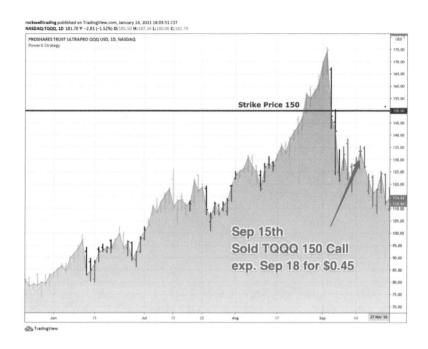

2 days later, on September 17th, I was able to buy back the call for $0.05.

So my profit is 0.45 - 0.05 = 0.40, and I'm able to reduce my cost basis for the stock to 147.61 - 0.40 = 147.21.

TQQQ still has a ways to go before I start making money again.

For now, I'm under water, and I need to keep selling premium to dig myself out of this hole.

But if TQQQ moves above my new cost basis of 147.21, I would make money.

Unfortunately, TQQQ had other plans….

Selling More Puts

On September 18, TQQQ closed at 116.48. This is the wrong direction!

So I'm adjusting my plan:

I decided to sell another Put with a strike price of 100.

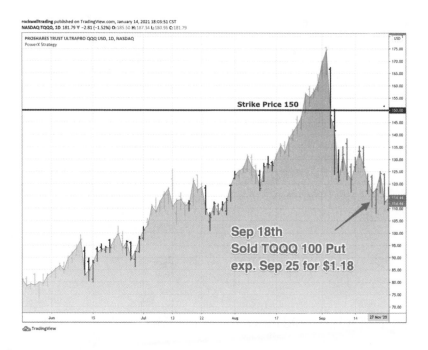

Here's my rational:

I already own 100 shares at a price of 150.

If TQQQ moves below $100, I would get assigned another 100 shares at $100.

So I would have 100 shares @ $150 and 100 shares @ $100.

This means that my average price for the shares is (150 + 100) / 2 = 125.

And I was able to collect some premium already:

Originally, I received $0.66 when selling my 150 Put.

I received another $1.73 when I sold the 150 Call.

And another $0.40 for selling another call.

Now I sold a put and received $1.18 in premium.

So the total premium I received thus far is 0.66 + 1.73 + 0.40 + 1.18 = 3.97.

When subtracting this from my average stock price at 125, I arrive at 125 - 3.97 = 121.03.

So if TQQQ would move above 121.03, I would start making money again!

Over the next few days, TQQQ is not going anywhere: It's moving a little bit higher, and then it's moving a little bit lower.

So on September 25th, I was able to buy back the 100 Put that I sold for $0.06.

My profit for this Put is 1.18 - 0.06 = 1.12.

Since I didn't get assigned, my cost basis is still 147.21. But since I made some more money selling premium, my cost basis is now 147.21 - 1.12 = 146.09.

I'm slowly moving my break-even point lower and lower....

On September 25th, I decided to sell another 100 Put expiring on October 2 for $2.40.

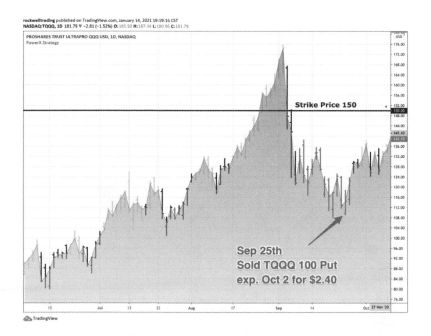

Just 3 days later, on September 28th, I can buy back this Put for $0.24. So my profit is 2.40 - 0.24 = 2.16.

With this profit, I'm lowering my cost basis to 146.09 - 2.16 = 143.93.

Selling Calls Again

Over the next few days, TQQQ is moving a little bit higher.

Not high enough for me to get out of this trade, but high enough for me to be able to sell calls again.

On October 1, I can sell a 150 Call expiring October 9th for $1.57.

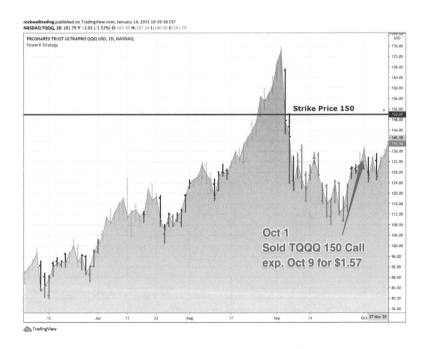

A few days later, on October 6th, I can buy back this call for $0.15.

My profit is 1.57 - 0.15 = 1.42, and my new cost basis is 143.93 - 1.42 = 142.51.

As you can see, it takes patience to dig yourself out of the hole, but it is possible!

Here's what happened next:

TQQQ is moving higher!

And on October 9th, I can sell the 150 Call expiring October 16 for $1.40.

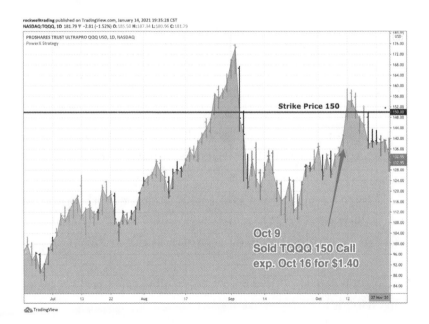

And then it finally happens:

TQQQ moves above 150!

But keep in mind: TQQQ needs to close above 150 on October 16 (expiration day). If it moves lower again, the calls expire worthless.

And that's what happened:

TQQQ stayed above 150 until October 14, just 2 days shy of expiration date.

But on October 16th, TQQQ is below 150 again, so we're still not out of the woods.

However, we can buy back our call for $0.40 and we make 1.40 - 0.40 = 1.00.

Our cost basis is now 142.51 - 1.00 = 141.51!

At this point, I could exit this trade and would make a small profit! And that might have been the smart thing to do.

But I have been in this trade for over one month now. I'm still bullish on TQQQ (which represents the NASDAQ) - and I'm determined to make a profit on this trade!

So on October 16, I'm selling a 155 Call expiring on October 23rd for $4.00.

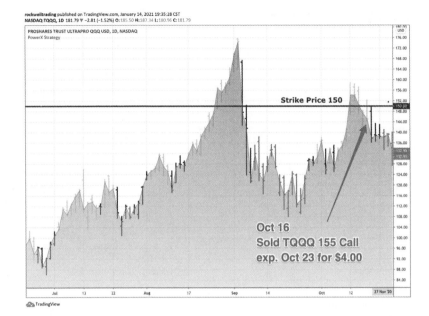

4 days later, on October 20th, I can buy back this call for $0.40, and I'm making a profit of 4.00 - 0.40 = 3.60.

My cost basis is now 141.51 - 3.60 = 137.91.

On October 21st, I'm selling a 150 Call expiring October 30th for $4.80.

TQQQ is moving lower again!!!!

Maybe I should have been smart and close the trade for a small profit when I could? - DANG!

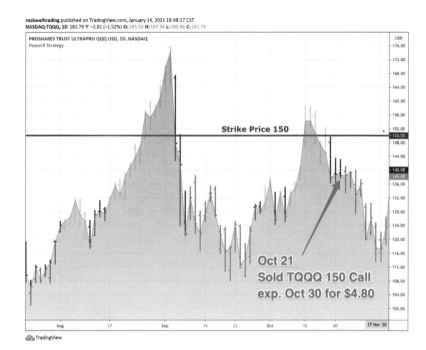

Since TQQQ is moving lower, I'm able to buy back this call on October 27 for $0.45.

So I collect another 4.80 - 0.45 = 4.35. My cost basis is now 137.91 - 4.35 = 133.56. If TQQQ moves above 133.56, I would make money!

Selling Puts - Again!

TQQQ keeps moving lower, and I can't get any more premium for calls.

I'm forced to sell puts - again!

So on October 30th, I'm selling a 100 Put expiring November 6th.

Will I ever be able to get out of this trade???

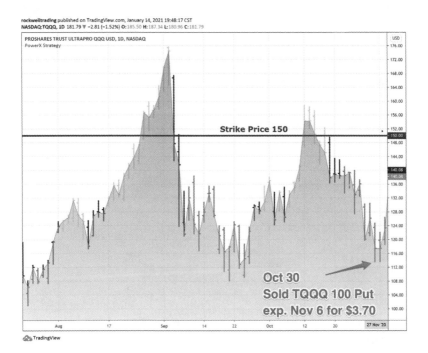

On November 3rd, I can buy back the put for $0.83 and a profit of 3.70 - 0.80 = 2.90. This helps me to reduce my cost basis to 133.56 - 2.90 = 130.66.

Finally: Selling Calls - for the last time?

Over the next few days, TQQQ is moving higher again, and I can sell more calls.

Since my cost basis is now at 130.66, I no longer have to sell 150 Calls. I can sell any strike price as long as it is above my cost basis.

On November 4th, I decided to sell the 148 Call expiring November 13 for $2.45.

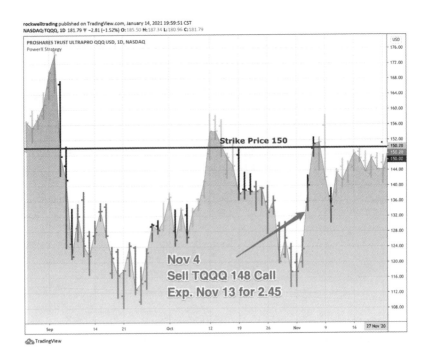

On November 13th, I can buy back the call for $0.10. My profit is 2.45 - 0.10 = 2.35, and my cost basis is now 128.31.

On the same day, November 13th, I can sell the 150 Call expiring November 20th for $2.60.

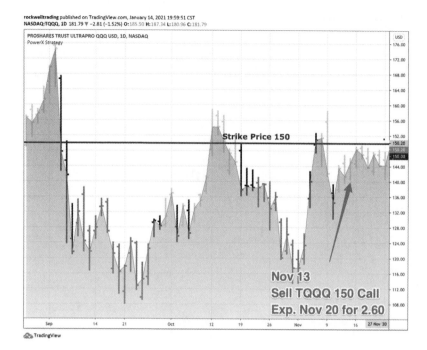

rockwelltrading published on TradingView.com, January 14, 2021 19:59:51 CST
NASDAQ:TQQQ, 1D 181.79 ▼ −2.81 (−1.52%) O:185.50 H:187.34 L:180.96 C:181.79

On November 20th, I was able to buy back the put for $0.20 for a profit of 2.60 - 0.20 = 2.40.

This reduced my cost basis to 128.31 - 2.40 = 125.91.

On the same day, I was able to sell the 150 Call expiring November 27 for $3.50.

And 7 days later...

... on November 27...

... after 82 days...

.... TQQQ closed above 150 and my shares got called away.

I didn't make any money on the shares, since I bought them for 150 and sold them again for 150.

But I collected **$2,759 in premium**.

By systematically selling calls and puts,

I successfully took a trade that was in trouble,

a trade on a stock that plummeted 39% after I entered,

a trade that had an unrealized loss of $4,190 at some point...

... and closed with $2,759 in profits.

Assignment Is All Part Of The Plan

Getting assigned is one of the things options traders fear the most.

But in reality, it is nothing that you should be worried about IF you understand what it means and have a plan for when it happens.

Some of my most profitable trades were the result of getting assigned.

This is why getting assigned is a major component of The Wheel Strategy.

So if you are not comfortable with getting assigned, this strategy may not be for you.

But if you take the time to learn the strategy, follow the steps outlined in this book, and practice it, you can have a lot of fun with this trading strategy!

Chapter 11

Ninja Tips and Tricks For Trading The Wheel

Are you excited about trading The Wheel?

I bet you are!

Because The Wheel Strategy gives you an edge in the market, and when done correctly, it's a "can't lose strategy" - almost!

However, when NOT executed correctly, you can experience some very serious losses.

So let me give you some Ninja tips and tricks for trading The Wheel Strategy, and some warnings!

Ninja Tip #1: The Most Important Question

When trading The Wheel, here's the most important question to ask yourself:

"Do I want to own the stock at the strike price?"

Always keep in mind that there is the risk of assignment.

If the stock moves below the strike price of the put that you sold, you will be forced to buy the stock at the strike price.

So are you ok owning the stock at that price point?

If the answer is YES, proceed.

If the answer is NO, then move on to the next stock.

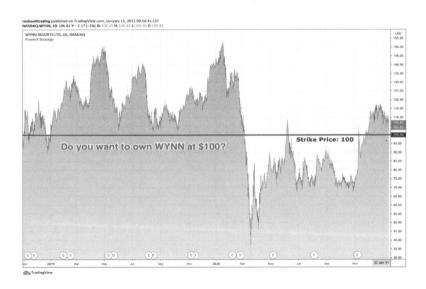

Ninja Tip #2: If It Is Too Good To Be True...

Sometimes you will see some GREAT opportunities.

Take a look at Novavax (NVAX):

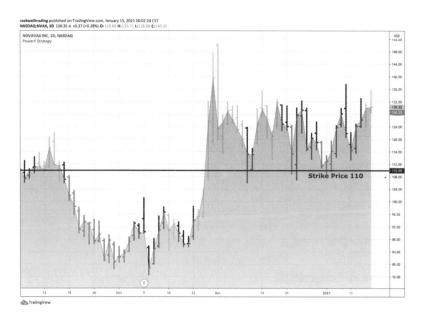

There is a lot of premium in the 100 Put expiring in 7 days.

In fact, there's so much premium that our Wheel Calculator shows you an annualized return of 71%!

Stock 1 ☐

Stock	**NVAX**
Stock Price ($)	130.57

Step 1: Selling Puts

Option Strike Price	110.00
Option Premium ($)	1.70
Expiration (date)	Jan 22, 2021 ⌄
Min Option Premium	0.72
Max Option Premium	0.96
Drop in %	16%
# Options to Trade	9
Premium Collected ($)	1,530
Days to Expiration (DTE)	7
Premium Per Day ($)	191
$ Needed to Buy Stock	99,000
Premium Annualized	71%

As you can see, the Wheel Calculator is highlighting it in YELLOW.

This is a warning sign!

You should expect annualized returns between 30% and 40%.

When you see 71%, and it's highlighted in yellow, it means that you need to double-check everything to make sure you didn't miss anything.

And sure enough:

A quick Google search reveals that Novavax (NVAX) is working on a Coronavirus vaccine:

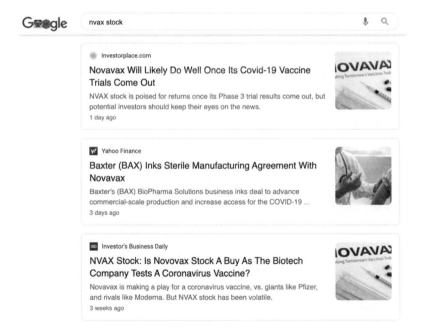

And yes, IF the trials go well, then Novavax might make a lot of money with the vaccine.

But if the trial fails, then this result could send Novavax sharply lower.

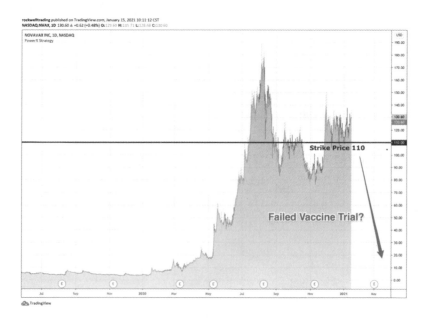

As you can see, NVAX has been trading around $4-6 until a few months ago.

So a failed trial might send NVAX down to those levels again.

Do you really want to own NVAX at $100 if it falls down to $4-6?

Always keep in mind: If it's too good to be true, it just might be.

Ninja Tip #3: Trade Weekly Options

You can trade options that expire weekly, and you can trade options that expire monthly.

You will find opportunities for both types of options.

I personally prefer trading weekly options because it gives me greater flexibility.

Here's why:

Let's say the price of a stock closes below the strike price at expiration, and you are getting assigned.

According to the rules, you would now sell a call.

With weekly options, you can sell a call that expires by the end of the week. And if the stock price closes ABOVE the strike price, your stocks will get called away, you're making money, and you can "spin the wheel" again and enter the next trade.

With monthly options, however, you will be stuck in the trade for the next 4 weeks, until the monthly options expire.

And it's much more difficult to predict what a stock will do within the next 4 weeks vs. trying to predict what the stock is more likely to do in 5 days.

Therefore, I highly recommend that you stick to WEEKLY options when trading The Wheel.

Ninja Tip #4: The Right Mindset

The Wheel Trading strategy is a strategy with an incredible high winning percentage.

I have been trading dozens and dozens of trades with The Wheel, and thus far I only had 1 losing trade (knock on wood!!!)

Therefore, my winning percentage is above 99%.

I don't know any other trading strategy that offers this kind of winning percentage.

It's very easy to get lulled in by the simplicity and effectiveness of this strategy.

But as a trader, you have to stay sharp and keep these 3 things in mind:

1. Only Trade With An Edge

Know your numbers!

Don't trade on hunches or just throw money at the market and *hope* it all works out. Practice, test, and verify your strategy before risking money.

Not only will this make you profitable, but it will give you confidence in your trading. Having an edge while trading will address many of the fears traders all experience at one time or another, especially the fear of losing money.

The Wheel Strategy is already a tested and verified strategy that will give you this edge. It is a time-tested, high probability strategy with more than a 95% win rate, making it tough to lose when implemented properly.

But take your time to learn the strategy and test it on a simulator to get comfortable and confident with the strategy, otherwise you could lose a lot of money!

2. Accept That Anything Can Happen With A Trade

Losses are part of the business.

If you haven't already accepted that, take a deep breath and do it right now. Because even if you have an edge, losses are still a part of trading.

There are times where no matter how disciplined you are, or how good you become at reading charts or picking stocks, there will be things outside of your control. You have no control of news that could come out. Accepting that there will be times that things don't work out will help you keep a level head when a tweet or headline ruins a trade.

We can only control whether it's a "good" loss or a "bad" loss.

A "good loss" is where you have followed and executed your plan perfectly, i.e. you did the best you could when finding the right stock, you picked the right strike price, you made sure that there's enough premium, and you executed the trade according to your plan. As long as YOU did everything right, but the trade resulted in a loss because the stock went crazy, this type of loss is a "good" loss.

A "bad loss" is a result of not following your trading plan. If you experience a loss because you didn't execute your plan properly, those are losses that YOU ARE in control of.

If, for example, you took a loss because you got too greedy and selected a strike price that was too close to the current price, then you were not following your plan. Or maybe you weren't disciplined enough. Or you didn't follow your plan and instead let emotions guide your decisions.

If you take a loss as a result of these reasons, this is considered a "bad" loss.

3. Know That It's A Numbers Game!

The Wheel Strategy gives you an edge. Use it to your advantage!

It's all about the big picture, not what happens on any single day. The long-term probability will work in your favor over time.

Casinos will lose big money from time to time to a player on a hot streak, but the reason casinos are still so profitable is that they know that over time they will get that back. They can't control the outcome of a single hand, on any single day, or week, but over time the math works out so they turn a profit year in and year out.

Think of yourself as "The House" of a casino. The odds are always in the favor of The House. If you stick to and execute a solid trading strategy systematically, the overall odds will be in your favor as well. Think about traders who don't trade with a strategy or trade with the proper mindset as gamblers in the casino. And even though every now and then a gambler can get lucky and win big, in the long run they will lose to The House.

Another way to think about this is to look at professional poker players.

Professional poker players know their odds. And they play their hands based on the odds, not based on their emotions. They don't let their emotions get the best of them and compound mistakes.

They will fold a hand the second they know when the odds are against them, instead of holding onto a hand until the end hoping they catch a longshot card.

They stick to a strategy just like professional traders do. They calculate the odds of hitting a card they need and compare these odds to the money in the pot (percentage of how much they will win compared to how much it will cost them to stay in a hand).

And that's what we do as professional traders:

We have an edge, we know our odds, and we use this edge to our advantage.

And both professional traders and professional poker players practice solid money management. A professional poker player knows the max he can lose in a single game, or at what percentage of profit he should cash out at.

Similarly, a professional trader knows the total amount of their trading account they can commit to a single position, and at what percentage in gains they should exit and take profits.

Most importantly, they both know it's a numbers game..

To summarize, these are 3 important principles for a proper trading mindset.

Always trade with an edge. If you do not have confidence in your edge, or if you don't believe you have an edge, then it's time to go back to the drawing board, practice trades on a simulator, or identify weaknesses. If you're trading with The Wheel Strategy, this is already a time tested strategy, so if you're not seeing results, go back and make sure you're applying the strategy correctly, and make adjustments if you need to.

Accept that anything can happen, so if you have a $5,000 account, don't do something like putting $2,500 into one trade where you could potentially lose half your account on one trade just because you THINK the markets are going to do something.

Finally, know that trading is a numbers game. You need to accept that winning or losing on an individual trade, or a series of trades will not make or break us.

Since this is a numbers game, trading with an edge will make us profitable over time.

When you approach trading with the proper mindset, you will actually be excited for the next trade after a loss, as opposed to feeling fear over the potential of another losing trade.

Ninja Tip #5: The Right Tools

There are 3 pillars of successful trading:

1. **A proven strategy,**
2. **Professional tools,**
3. **The right mindset.**

You already know a proven trading strategy that gives you an edge. And on the previous pages we talked about the right mindset.

So let's talk about professional tools for a moment:

Professional tools make your life easier and eliminate mistakes.

Think about it this way: When trading, you're trading against the brightest minds in the world! You are trading against professional traders who use sophisticated tools to scan the markets, find the best opportunities, calculate their odds, and execute the trades.

If you don't have the right tools, it's like trying to win a NASCAR race riding a llama!

You have no chance. No matter how well you can ride llamas… if you are trying to compete against professional drivers in sophisticated race cars that have been fine tuned to the track, the road conditions and the driver - you will NEVER win.

I personally would NEVER trade without my tool PowerX Optimizer.

If you want to win "the game of games," then I highly recommend that you take a look at the PowerX Optimizer.

I did a video for you in which I show you how I use this tool in my own trading every day to find the best opportunities and make the best decisions.

You can watch the video here: myTradingRoutine.com

That's it!

- You now know a proven trading strategy that gives you an edge in the market.

- You know the exact steps to take to find highly profitable trades.

- You know how to rescue a trade that's in trouble.

- You know about the right mindset for trading.

- And you know where to find the best tools for your trading.

At this point, it's a matter of TAKING ACTION and GETTING STARTED.

Nothing will happen unless you use the techniques and strategies that I gave you to start trading.

Trade on a simulator first!

Get experience and see for yourself how powerful this strategy is.

Once you are comfortable with the strategy, start trading it with real money.

I would love to hear from you about your success!

All the best in your trading,

Markus

Bonus Resources

We have some very cool tools and resources for you.

We created a page where you can access all these tools, and we update it frequently.

WheelStrategyBook.com/bonus

On this page, you will find:

- The charting software that I personally use

- The tool that finds the best trades for The Wheel for you - automatically

- The broker that I use for trading The Wheel

- Videos with updates, more tips and tricks,

- ... and much more!

Go there now to get the additional resources we have for you:

WheelStrategyBook.com/bonus

The PowerX Strategy - A Powerful Trading Strategy for Stocks and Options

The PowerX Strategy is a systematic, repeatable and consistent swing trading strategy for stocks and options.

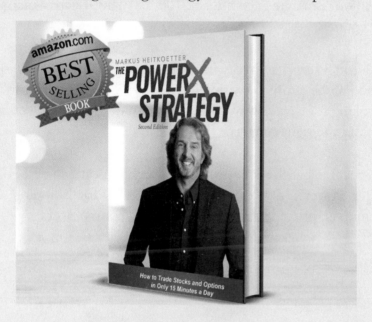

This trend following strategy can be traded in bullish or bear markets, with stock or options.

Using a time tested money management system, it takes the possibility of account destroying losses off the table, when implemented correctly.

You can start with as little as $5,000 to trade options, and $10,000 if you want to trade stocks.

This powerful growth strategy only requires 15-20 minutes per day, without having to sit in front of your computer, watching every tick of a chart.

With the PowerX Strategy, I'm looking for a ROI of 60% without a margin account, and 100-120% ROI with a margin account.

As you'll see, that even with worse than a 50% win rate, you can still be profitable using The PowerX Strategy. If you're looking for a great way to grow your trading account, you've found the right strategy.

Get a free hardback copy of my Amazon Best Selling book, The PowerX Strategy, just cover $4.95 for shipping & handling: https://www.rockwelltrading.com/powerx

The PowerX Optimizer - Automatically Find The Best Stocks and Options For "The Wheel"

You know how powerful The Wheel strategy is.

As I explained in the previous chapters, the biggest challenge is to find the best stocks to trade for The Wheel.

And that's why I developed this tool that makes it easy for you:

The PowerX Optimizer can dramatically help you become a successful and profitable trader.

Especially since this is one of the easiest tools you could ever have at your disposal.

Seriously. With just a few clicks of my mouse, you get a list of both conservative and aggressive Wheel Trades, without hours of hunting through thousands of stocks. You will get the best strike prices and expirations to trade.

And the built-in Wheel Calculator shows you exactly what to expect from each trade and when to take profits.

I would never trade The Wheel strategy without this powerful tool. I use it every day in my trading.

We're making the software better and better and to this point, I've invested nearly $1,000,000 into its development...and it's been worth every penny.

If you'd like to take a no risk tour of the software, you can schedule it here to check it out:
https://www.rockwelltrading.com/pxotour